A Symphony of British Music

Une symphonie de musique britannique

London 2012 Olympic Games Closing Ceremony
12 August 2012

Cérémonie de clôture des Jeux Olympiques de Londres 2012
Le 12 août 2012

Please note, the Ceremony includes strobe lighting, pyrotechnics and lasers.

Veuillez noter que la Cérémonie inclut des éclairages stroboscopiques, des dispositifs pyrotechniques et des lasers.

HRH Prince Henry of Wales

The London 2012 Olympic Games have been extraordinary. They will stay in the hearts and minds of people all over the world for a very long time to come.

I congratulate all the athletes who have competed. They have shown us that there are few boundaries to human endeavour. Demonstrating great pride in representing their countries, these men and women have inspired everyone with their determination and their sportsmanship.

The Games have brought together athletes and spectators from very different cultures, backgrounds and faiths, and from every corner of the planet. Their collaboration and spirit represent a magnificent force for positive change.

You have captured the imagination of the world.

None of this would have been possible without the tens of thousands of people, both in the United Kingdom and around the world, who have prepared the teams for competition as well as those who have brought the Games in London to fruition.

So many of these have been volunteers and their efforts have been supreme. They have not received medals, but they assuredly share in the triumph of the London 2012 Olympic Games.

Les Jeux Olympiques de Londres 2012 ont été extraordinaires. Ils resteront dans les mémoires et dans les cœurs de par le monde pendant très longtemps.

Je félicite tous les athlètes qui ont participé à la compétition. Ils nous ont montré qu'il y a peu de limites à ce dont l'être humain est capable. Montrant une immense fierté à représenter leur pays, ces hommes et ces femmes ont été une inspiration pour tous par leur détermination et leur esprit sportif.

Ces Jeux ont rassemblé des athlètes et des spectateurs venus de tous les horizons, avec des origines, des cultures et des religions très diverses. Leur esprit de collaboration et leur passion sont une magnifique force de changement.

Vous avez captivé l'attention de toute la planète.

Rien de tout cela n'aurait été possible sans les dizaines de milliers de personnes, tant au Royaume-Uni que dans le reste du monde, qui ont aidé les équipes à se préparer ainsi que ceux qui ont mené à bien l'organisation des Jeux, à Londres.

Nombre d'entre eux étaient bénévoles et ils se sont dépensés sans compter. Ils n'ont pas reçu de médaille mais ils ont sans conteste part au triomphe des Jeux Olympiques de Londres 2012.

Jacques Rogge

President of the International Olympic Committee
Président du Comité International Olympique

It has been 16 days since the Olympic Flame ignited the cauldron here at the magnificent Olympic Stadium. Tonight the Flame will be extinguished, bringing a close to the Games of the XXX Olympiad.

What won't be extinguished are all the special moments and memories created during London 2012, in particular the exceptional performances of the world's best athletes.

We are here tonight to celebrate their achievements and applaud all the athletes who came to London to compete in a spirit of excellence, friendship and respect. It is thanks to them that the London 2012 Olympic Games will long be remembered as a benchmark for sporting excellence.

Of course, the Games would not have been such a success without the outstanding work of a host of different individuals and organisations. The passion for and support of the Games shown by the people of London and the United Kingdom deserve special praise as they helped create a unique and exciting environment for the athletes, visitors to the city and the billions of viewers watching around the world.

Thank you to the governments of London and the United Kingdom for your unwavering support of the organisation of the London Games.

Our friends at the London 2012 Organising Committee should also take great pride in all that they accomplished. Your work from the very outset was simply outstanding.

I would also like to extend my highest praise to the unsung heroes of any edition of the Olympic Games: the volunteers. Your dedication, enthusiasm and contribution to London 2012 did not go unnoticed. Without you none of this could have happened!

Finally, thank you to the International Sports Federations and National Olympic Committees for supporting the athletes and allowing them to do what they do best for the enjoyment of billions around the world.

After experiencing so many highs over the last 16 days, it is with some sadness that we bring these Games to a close. But London has been a gracious host and the Games will unquestionably leave a long and lasting legacy for the city, country and Olympic Movement.

Thank you, London! And see you in Rio in 2016!

Cela fait maintenant 16 jours que la flamme olympique a embrasé la vasque de ce magnifique stade olympique. Ce soir, la flamme va s'éteindre et le rideau tombera sur les Jeux de la XXXe Olympiade.

Mais ne s'effaceront pas de notre souvenir tous ces moments si particuliers vécus pendant les Jeux, et notamment les performances exceptionnelles des meilleurs athlètes du monde.

Nous sommes ici ce soir pour célébrer leurs exploits et applaudir tous les athlètes venus à Londres en quête d'excellence, concourir dans un esprit d'amitié et de respect. C'est grâce à eux que les Jeux Olympiques de 2012 à Londres resteront longtemps dans les mémoires comme un modèle d'excellence sportive.

Naturellement, les Jeux n'auraient pas été une telle réussite sans le travail extraordinaire d'une pléiade d'hommes et de femmes ainsi que d'organisations. La passion et le soutien manifestés pour les Jeux par la population de Londres et du Royaume-Uni méritent une mention spéciale car ils auront permis de créer une ambiance unique et exaltante pour les athlètes, les visiteurs et les milliards de téléspectateurs dans le monde entier.

Aux autorités de Londres et du Royaume-Uni, je dis merci pour votre soutien indéfectible à l'organisation des Jeux.

Nos amis du comité d'organisation des Jeux de 2012 à Londres doivent également se sentir très fiers de tout ce qu'ils ont accompli. Votre travail depuis le début a tout simplement été remarquable.

J'aimerais en outre adresser mes plus vives félicitations aux héros de l'ombre de toute édition des Jeux Olympiques, à vous les volontaires. Votre dévouement, votre enthousiasme et votre contribution aux Jeux de 2012 ne sont pas passés inaperçus. Sans vous, rien de tout cela n'aurait été possible !

Enfin, je remercie les Fédérations Internationales de sport et les Comités Nationaux Olympiques d'avoir soutenu les athlètes et de leur avoir permis de faire ce qu'ils font de mieux pour le plus grand plaisir de milliards de fans dans le monde.

Après avoir vécu tant de grands moments au cours de ces 16 derniers jours, c'est non sans une pointe de tristesse que nous devons clore ces Jeux. Mais Londres nous aura offert une gracieuse hospitalité et les Jeux laisseront incontestablement un héritage durable à la ville, au pays et au Mouvement olympique.

Merci Londres ! Et rendez-vous en 2016 à Rio !

Sebastian Coe

Chair, London 2012 Organising Committee
Président du Comité d'organisation de Londres 2012

As the athletes gather for the Closing Ceremony, and the world gets ready to say farewell to the Games of the XXX Olympiad, the time has come to say goodbye and thank you.

The Games have brought the world a little closer, lifted our hopes and horizons, and reminded us of our common humanity – that we are world citizens and that we strive for a better future for mankind.

Together we've delivered an Olympic Games for our world and for our times. Games for everyone – people of all faiths, cultures and backgrounds – in a time of conflict. Games that have connected millions of young people around the world directly with sport and the Olympic values. Games focused on excellence without extravagance, in the global financial downturn. And Games delivered sustainably and responsibly, with a major emphasis on protecting the environment and scarce natural resources.

We thank and pay tribute to the British people, whose generosity of spirit and passion for sport made these Games possible. As well as the best athletes, we had the best volunteers, our Games Makers, who dedicated themselves to doing something positive for the world's athletes, for their country, and for the world.

Thank you to the IOC for entrusting these Games to us – we hope we have met the high expectations for London 2012. Thank you to our wonderful partners and sponsors, for believing and investing in our vision for change. And thank you to the heroic men and women in uniform for keeping us from harm.

And above all, thank you to the athletes. When the world recalls London 2012, thoughts will return to a special time and place, to a journey through the mists of time to a 'green and pleasant land'. We'll remember inspiring accounts of the achievements of the athletes, stories of epic sporting contests, and extraordinary performances that captured the imagination of people everywhere, united our diverse planet and inspired a generation.

Young people will think differently about the world after London 2012, knowing that it's possible to achieve great things – to triumph over adversity, to change their circumstances and to believe in themselves. This will keep the Olympic ideal alive for future generations, until hopes of staging the Olympic Games begin to stir again, and we dream once more of welcoming you back to the 'Isles of Wonder'.

Les athlètes se réunissent pour la Cérémonie de Clôture et le monde s'apprête à dire adieu aux Jeux de la XXXe Olympiade. Le moment est venu de dire au revoir et merci.

Les Jeux ont rapproché la planète, ont revivifié nos espoirs et nos horizons et nous ont rappelé notre commune humanité : nous sommes des citoyens du monde nous efforçant de créer un meilleur avenir pour les hommes.

Ensemble nous avons produit des Jeux Olympiques de notre monde et de notre temps. Des Jeux pour tous, de toutes confessions, cultures et origines, dans une période de conflit. Des Jeux qui ont tissé des liens entre des millions de jeunes dans le monde et le sport et les valeurs olympiques. Des Jeux concentrés sur l'excellence sans extravagance, sur fond de récession économique mondiale. Des Jeux produits de manière durable et responsable, portant l'accent sur la protection de l'environnement et des ressources naturelles limitées.

Nous disons merci et rendons hommage au peuple britannique, dont la générosité d'esprit et la passion pour le sport ont rendu les Jeux possibles. En plus des meilleurs athlètes, nous avions les meilleurs bénévoles, nos Games Makers, qui se sont consacrés à apporter une contribution positive, pour les athlètes internationaux, leur pays et pour le monde.

Nous remercions le CIO de nous avoir confié ces Jeux ; nous espérons avoir été à la hauteur des attentes à l'égard de Londres 2012. Merci à nos partenaires et sponsors pour avoir cru et avoir investi dans notre vision du changement. Merci aussi aux héros en uniforme d'avoir su veiller à la sécurité de tous.

Enfin, surtout, merci aux athlètes. En repensant à Londres 2012, le monde retiendra un temps et un lieu extraordinaires, un voyage à travers le temps sur des « douces terres verdoyantes ». Nous retiendrons les récits de victoires exemplaires des athlètes, de compétitions sportives prodigieuses et de prouesses extraordinaires qui ont captivé le monde entier, unifié notre planète si diverse et inspiré une génération.

Les jeunes verront le monde différemment après Londres 2012, forts de l'idée qu'il est possible d'accomplir de grandes choses : triompher de l'adversité, changer sa vie et croire en soi-même. C'est ce qui entretiendra la flamme de l'idéal olympique pour les générations à venir, jusqu'à ce que l'espoir d'organiser les Jeux renaisse et que nous rêvions de vous accueillir de nouveau sur nos « Îles aux Merveilles ».

Rt Hon David Cameron MP

Prime Minister
Premier ministre

The races have been run, the lengths have been swum, the medals have been awarded. This has been a truly spectacular Olympics, lit up by incredible sporting moments and an outpouring of national pride.

We've seen a new generation of heroes step into the spotlight – medal-winners who have inspired children around the world to try their best and keep trying until they succeed.

Then there are the heroes who made their mark behind the scenes: the volunteers who gave up their time to welcome the world to London; the workers who made these Games such a success. I want to thank each and every one of them.

But though the Games are drawing to a close, this isn't the end of the story – far from it. This is just the start of the next chapter, where we build on the success of the Games to leave a lasting legacy in London and across the United Kingdom – a legacy that will be measured in new investment in our cities and a new passion for sport in our communities.

At the start of this Olympics our ambition was simple: the biggest possible celebration, the greatest possible participation and the best possible legacy. I don't think anyone can deny that London 2012 has achieved all of this and more.

Les lignes d'arrivée ont été franchies, les longueurs nagées, les médailles distribuées. Cette olympiade fut vraiment spectaculaire, marquée de grands moments de sport et de fierté nationale.

Nous avons vu s'avancer sous les feux de la rampe une nouvelle génération de héros, champions médaillés qui incitent tous les enfants du monde à faire de leur mieux et à persévérer jusqu'au succès.

Et puis il y a ces héros qui ont œuvré en coulisse : les bénévoles qui ont donné de leur temps pour accueillir à Londres le monde entier et les travailleurs qui ont assuré le succès des Jeux. J'adresse mes remerciements à chacun d'entre eux.

Si les Jeux tirent à leur fin, l'histoire ne s'arrête pas pour autant. Loin de là ! Ce n'est que le début d'un nouveau chapitre, où nous capitalisons sur la réussite des Jeux pour laisser un patrimoine durable à Londres et dans tout le Royaume-Uni : cet héritage se mesurera aux nouveaux investissements dans nos villes et à une passion renouvelée pour le sport dans nos communautés.

Au début de ces olympiades, notre ambition était simple : la plus grande fête possible, avec la participation la plus large possible et le plus bel héritage possible. Je crois qu'il est indéniable que les Jeux de Londres 2012 ont atteint cet objectif — et plus encore.

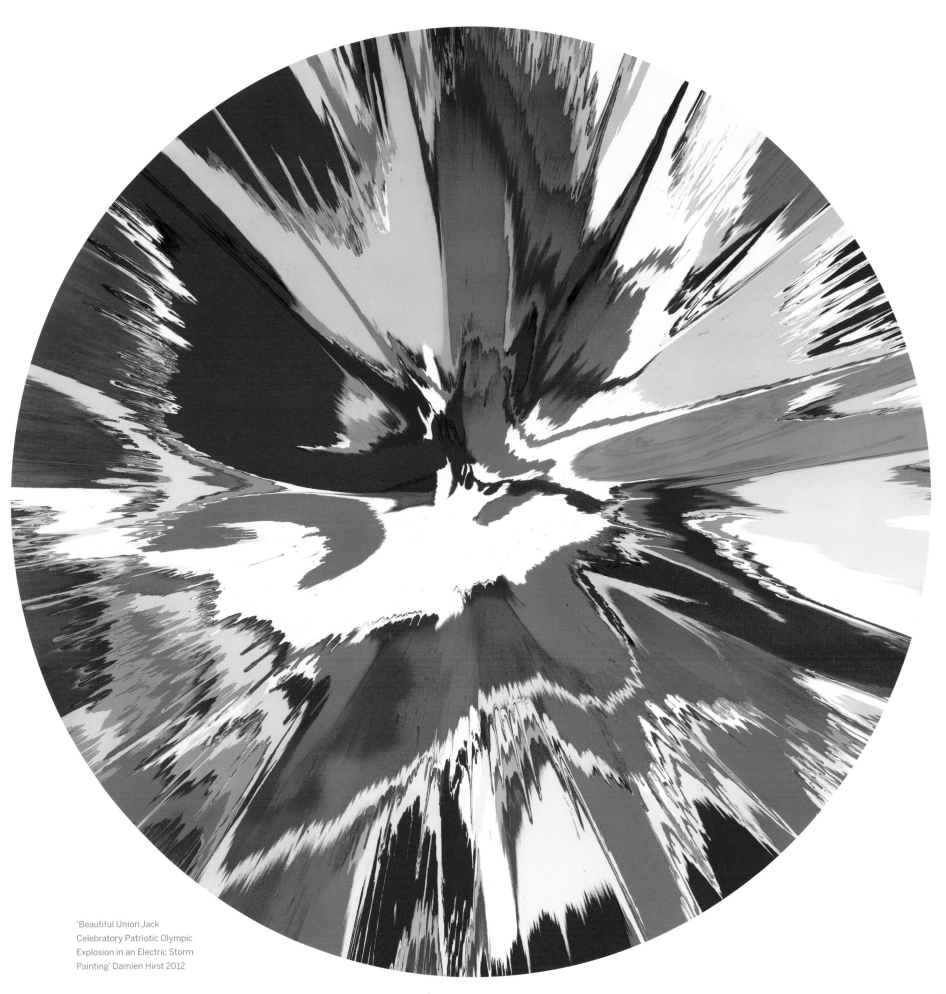

'Beautiful Union Jack
Celebratory Patriotic Olympic
Explosion in an Electric Storm
Painting' Damien Hirst 2012

Read all about it...

...read all about it

The city wakes: everyday, working, newsprint grey London. But the headlines are the work of the English poetic imagination – from medieval Chaucer to contemporary Carol Ann Duffy. And as the city unwraps itself amid the cacophony and chaos of rush hour, we reveal the British character in snapshot – a celebration of irony, irreverence and, most of all, imagination.

La ville s'éveille : le Londres du quotidien, du travail, gris papier journal. Mais ce qui fait la une, c'est l'imagination poétique anglaise, de Chaucer au Moyen Âge à Carol Ann Duffy de nos jours. Et alors que la cité se déploie dans la cacophonie et le chaos de l'heure de pointe, se révèle l'âme britannique en un coup d'œil : une célébration de l'ironie, de l'irrévérence et, surtout, de l'imagination.

'Sometimes a thousand twangling instruments will hum about mine ears'

The Tempest, William Shakespeare

« *Parfois des milliers d'instruments retentissent confusément à mes oreilles* »
La Tempête, William Shakespeare

God Save the Queen

God save our gracious Queen!
Long live our noble Queen!
God save the Queen!
Send her victorious,
Happy and glorious,
Long to reign over us,
God save the Queen.

Thy choicest gifts in store
On her be pleased to pour,
Long may she reign.
May she defend our laws,
And ever give us cause,
To sing with heart and voice,
God save the Queen.

A fanfare by The Household
Division Ceremonial State
Band welcomes...
**His Royal Highness
Prince Henry of Wales**
and

Jacques Rogge
President of the
International Olympic
Committee

Que Dieu protège la Reine
*Le Household Division
Ceremonial State Band
accueille en fanfare...*
**Son Altesse Royale le
prince Henry de Galles**
et

Jacques Rogge
*Président du Comité
Olympique International*

*Que Dieu protège notre gracieuse Reine,
Longue vie à notre noble Reine,
Que Dieu protège la Reine !
Rends-la victorieuse,
Rayonnante et glorieuse,
Que soit long son règne sur nous,
Que Dieu protège la Reine !*

*Qu'il Te plaise de lui accorder
Tes bienfaits les plus rares ;
Puisse-t-elle régner longuement ;
Puisse-t-elle défendre nos lois
Et nous donner toujours raison
De chanter avec cœur et à pleine voix :
Que Dieu protège la Reine !*

'There's always something happening and it's usually quite loud'

SIR EDWARD ELGAR 1857–1934 Composer lived here 1890–1891

It's party time on the streets of London. Grey bursts into a celebratory spectrum of colour. Rain clouds are blasted away in a centrifugal explosion of red, white and blue – Damien Hirst's giant spin painting epitomises the dynamic, anarchic energy of British Pop Art.

C'est l'heure de la fête dans les rues de Londres. Soudain, la grisaille laisse place à une explosion de couleurs pétillantes. Les nuages sont chassés par un tourbillon de rouge, blanc et bleu : la peinture spirale géante de Damien Hirst est à l'image de l'énergie anarchique du pop art britannique.

'East End boys and West End girls'

Waterloo Sunset
Coucher de soleil sur Waterloo

Sunset transforms the domes and spires of the London skyline into a surreal, supersaturated, luminous funfair that's balanced and bounced on by clown-headed acrobatic city businessmen. A shimmering river of children weave their way through, oblivious to the absurdities of the antics above.

Le coucher de soleil transforme les coupoles et aiguilles du ciel londonien en un parc de jeux surréaliste, sursaturé et flamboyant avec lequel jouent, dans une chorégraphie acrobatique, des business men à tête de clown de la City. Un flot scintillant d'enfants se fraie un passage, sans se préoccuper des singeries absurdes au-dessus de lui.

14

'As long as I gaze
on Waterloo sunset,
I am in paradise'

Parade of Athletes
Défilé des athlètes

'One day like this'

The Olympic Games offer a unique opportunity to bring out the best in individuals and unite us all. This evening, we celebrate the 10,490 athletes from more than 200 nations whose exceptional endeavours and commitment to the Olympic values – excellence, friendship and respect – have been an inspiration to young and old across the world.

Les Jeux Olympiques offrent une occasion unique de montrer le meilleur de chacun et de nous unir tous. Ce soir, nous célébrons les 10 490 athlètes de plus de 200 nations différentes dont les efforts et l'attachement aux valeurs des Jeux – excellence, amitié et respect – ont été une source d'inspiration pour les jeunes et moins jeunes à travers le monde.

Greece > Afghanistan > Albania > Algeria >

American Samoa > Andorra > Angola > Antigua and Barbuda >

Argentina > Armenia > Aruba > Australia > Austria > Azerbaijan >

Bahamas > Bahrain > Bangladesh > Barbados > Belarus >

Belgium > Belize > Benin > Bermuda > Bhutan > Bolivia > Bosnia and Herzegovina >

Botswana > Brazil > British Virgin Islands > Brunei Darussalam >

Bulgaria > Burkina Faso > Burundi >

Central African Republic > Cambodia > Cameroon > Canada > Cape Verde > Cayman Islands >

Chad > Chile > People's Republic of China > Colombia >

Comoros > Congo > Cook Islands > Costa Rica > Côte d'Ivoire >

Croatia > Cuba > Cyprus > Czech Republic > Democratic People's Republic of Korea >

Democratic Republic of the Congo > Denmark > Djibouti > Dominica > Dominican Republic >

Ecuador > Egypt > El Salvador > Equatorial Guinea > Eritrea > Estonia > Ethiopia >

Fiji > Finland > Former Yugoslav Republic of Macedonia > France > Gabon >

Gambia > Georgia > Germany > Ghana > Grenada > Guam > Guatemala > Guinea >

Guinea-Bissau > Guyana > Haiti > Honduras >

Hong Kong, China > Hungary > Iceland > Independent Olympic Athletes > India > Indonesia >

Islamic Republic of Iran > Iraq > Ireland > Israel > Italy > Jamaica > Japan > Jordan >

Kazakhstan > Kenya > Kiribati > Republic of Korea > Kuwait > Kyrgyzstan > Lao People's Democratic Republic >

Liechtenstein > Lithuania > Marshall Islands > Mauritania > Monaco > Montenegro > Morocco > Mozambique >

Latvia > Lebanon > Lesotho > Liberia > Libya > Malaysia > Maldives > Mali > Malta > Mongolia >

Luxembourg > Madagascar > Malawi > Federated States of Micronesia > Republic of Moldova > Niger > Nigeria >

Mauritius > Mexico > New Zealand > Nicaragua > Papua New Guinea > Paraguay > Russian Federation > San Marino >

Myanmar > Namibia > Nauru > Nepal > Netherlands > Panama > Romania > Samoa > Singapore > Slovakia > Slovenia >

Norway > Oman > Pakistan > Palau > Palestine > Qatar > Sierra Leone > Chinese Taipei > Tonga >

Peru > Philippines > Poland > Portugal > Puerto Rico > Saint Vincent and the Grenadines > Timor-Leste > Togo > Tuvalu >

Rwanda > Saint Kitts and Nevis > Saint Lucia > Serbia > Seychelles > Sri Lanka > Turkmenistan > United States of America >

Sao Tome and Principe > Saudi Arabia > Senegal > South Africa > Spain > Syrian Arab Republic > Thailand > Turkey > Vanuatu > Venezuela > Vietnam >

Solomon Islands > Somalia > Swaziland > Sweden > Switzerland > Tunisia > United Arab Emirates > Uruguay > Uzbekistan >

Sudan > Suriname > United Republic of Tanzania > Uganda > Ukraine > Virgin Islands > Yemen > Zambia > Zimbabwe > Great Britain

Tajikistan > Trinidad and Tobago >

Grèce > Afghanistan > Albanie > Algérie >

Samoa américaines > Andorre > Angola > Antigua-et-Barbuda >

Argentine > Arménie > Aruba > Australie > Autriche > Azerbaïdjan > Bahamas > Bahreïn >

Bangladesh > Barbade > Bélarus > Belgique > Belize > Bénin > Bermudes >

Bhoutan > Bolivie > Bosnie-Herzégovine > Botswana > Brésil > Îles Vierges britanniques > Brunéi Darussalam > Bulgarie >

Burkina Faso > Burundi > Cambodge > Cameroun > Canada > Cap-Vert > Îles Caïmans >

Congo > Îles Cook >

République populaire de Chine > Colombie > Comores >

Costa Rica > Côte d'Ivoire > Croatie > Cuba > Chypre > République tchèque >

République centrafricaine > Tchad > Chili >

République populaire démocratique de Corée > République démocratique du Congo >

Équateur > Égypte > El Salvador > Guinée équatoriale > Érythrée > Estonie >

Danemark > Djibouti > Dominique > République dominicaine >

Éthiopie > Fidji > Finlande > Ex-République yougoslave de Macédoine > France > Gabon > Gambie > Géorgie >

Guinée > Guinée-Bissau > Guyana > Haïti > Honduras >

Allemagne > Ghana > Grenade > Guam > Guatemala >

Hong Kong, Chine > Hongrie > Islande > Athlètes olympiques indépendants > Inde >

Indonésie > République islamique d'Iran > Iraq > Irlande > Israël > Italie > Jamaïque >

Japon > Jordanie > Kazakhstan > Kenya > Kiribati > République de Corée >

Koweït > Kirghizistan > République démocratique populaire lao > Lettonie >

Liban > Lesotho > Libéria > Libye > Liechtenstein > Lituanie > Luxembourg > Madagascar > Malawi > Malaisie >

Maldives > Mali > Malte > Îles Marshall > Mauritanie > Maurice > Mexique > États fédérés de Micronésie >

Nigéria > Norvège > Oman > Pakistan > Palaos > Palestine > Panama >

République de Moldova > Monaco > Mongolie > Monténégro > Maroc > Mozambique > Myanmar > Namibie > Nauru >

Népal > Pays-Bas > Nouvelle-Zélande > Nicaragua > Niger >

États-Unis d'Amérique >

Slovénie > Îles Salomon > Saint-Vincent-et-les-Grenadines >

Tadjikistan > République-Unie de Tanzanie > Somalie > Samoa >

Papouasie-Nouvelle-Guinée > Paraguay >

Pologne > Portugal > Porto Rico > Qatar > Pérou > Philippines >

Vietnam > Îles Vierges des États-Unis > Yémen > Zambie >

Tuvalu > Ouganda > Ukraine > Émirats arabes unis >

Trinité-et-Tobago > Tunisie > Turquie > Turkménistan >

Thaïlande > Timor-Leste > Togo > Tonga >

Afrique du Sud > Espagne > Sri Lanka > Soudan > Suriname > Swaziland >

Suède > Suisse > République arabe syrienne >

Serbie > Seychelles > Sao Tomé-et-Principe > Arabie Saoudite > Sénégal >

Fédération de Russie > Rwanda > Saint-Kitts-et-Nevis > Sainte-Lucie >

Sierra Leone > Singapour > Slovaquie >

Saint-Marin > Roumanie >

Chinese Taipei >

Zimbabwe > Grande-Bretagne

Uruguay > Ouzbékistan > Vanuatu > Venezuela >

Here Comes the Sun
Voici le soleil

Men's Marathon Victory Ceremony

The longest odyssey. A winning smile at the end of 26 miles and 385 yards. In time-honoured tradition, the Men's Marathon Victory Ceremony brings down the curtain on the Games' medal-giving.

IOC Athletes' Commission

This evening, we recognise the four newly elected members of the IOC's Athletes' Commission, who represent athletes within the Olympic Movement and uphold their rights and obligations.

Volunteer Recognition

You don't have to win a medal to be a hero. Tonight, the athletes and all of us recognise the 70,000 Games Maker volunteers whose energy, enthusiasm and remarkable dedication has contributed to the success of London 2012.

Cérémonie de la victoire du marathon hommes
La plus longue des odyssées. Un sourire de gagnant au bout des 42,195 km. Comme le veut la tradition, la cérémonie de victoire du marathon hommes marque la fin des remises de médailles.

La commission des athlètes du CIO
Ce soir, nous rendons hommage aux quatre nouveaux élus de la Commission des athlètes du CIO qui représentent les athlètes au sein du Mouvement Olympique et font respecter leurs droits et devoirs.

Hommage aux bénévoles
Pas besoin de gagner une médaille pour être un héros. Ce soir, les athlètes et nous tous saluons les 70 000 Games Makers bénévoles dont l'énergie, l'enthousiasme et le remarquable dévouement ont contribué au succès de Londres 2012.

'sun, here it comes', sun, 'un, 'uns, sun, 'uns,

XXX Olympiad London 2012

'Is this the real life?'

Over the past 50 years British pop music has underscored memories and moments in lives all around the globe. Imagine a celestial radio tuning through the unforgettable lyrics and melodies that immediately transport the listener through time and place. But this is no chronologically packaged back-to-back catalogue of greatest hits by greatest Brits – more a spontaneous, unpredictable synergy of styles with a spectacular sense of adventure.

Au cours des 50 dernières années, la pop britannique s'est liée aux souvenirs et moments de la vie de millions de personnes de par le monde. Imaginez une radio cosmique diffusant les paroles et musiques inoubliables qui transportent instantanément l'auditeur à travers le temps et l'espace. Mais ce n'est pas un catalogue chronologique des meilleurs tubes made in UK, plutôt une synergie spontanée et imprévisible de styles avec un sens spectaculaire de l'aventure.

'I'm a dreamer, but I'm not the only one'

The simple and essential message 'imagine peace' is as vital today as it ever was. It's this spirit that underlies the Olympic Truce movement. In 2011, a United Nations resolution urged the observance of a global truce during the London 2012 Olympic and Paralympic Games. Imagining peace, together, could be the first step towards making it a reality.

Le message simple et primordial « imagine la paix » est aussi vital aujourd'hui que jamais. C'est l'esprit qui sous-tend le mouvement de la Trêve Olympique. En 2011, une résolution des Nations Unies a demandé le respect d'une trêve mondiale pour la durée des Jeux Olympiques et Paralympiques de Londres 2012. Imaginer la paix, ensemble, pourrait être le premier pas vers sa concrétisation.

'From Soho down to Brighton'

'I wish that I could be that bird and fly

Photos © Nick Knight

Music and fashion – twin peaks of our cultural output, inextricably linked down the decades. From Mod to rock, punk to Brit pop, British designers are renowned for capturing the sound of the suburbs in the look of the catwalk. David Bowie's lyrics scorn fashion's blind followers. We celebrate the innovative leaders of British fashion.

Musique et mode : jumelles incontournables et inséparables, fruits de notre culture, qui dansent ensemble depuis des décennies. Du style mod au rock, du punk à la Brit pop, les créateurs de Grande-Bretagne sont connus pour mettre les rythmes urbains sur les podiums des défilés. Les paroles de David Bowie dédaignent les suiveurs, victimes de la mode. Nous célébrons les champions novateurs de la mode britannique.

'...away from here'

'Two lost souls swimming in a fish bowl'

'We are the goon squad and we're coming to town, beep-beep'

26

'Check it out now, the funk soul brother'

Our pavements may be grey, but by night we dream in iridescent colour. Elements of daily life are seen through the surreal prism of psychedelic song lyrics. Expect the unexpected as we celebrate British individuality and freedom of spirit – the essence of the English eccentric.

Nos trottoirs sont peut-être gris mais, la nuit, nos rêves ont les couleurs de l'arc-en-ciel. Les petites choses de la vie quotidienne sont vues à travers le prisme surréaliste des paroles de chanson psychédéliques. Attendez-vous à l'inattendu : nous fêtons l'individualité et la liberté d'esprit britanniques, l'essence même de l'excentrique à l'anglaise.

'All the colours of the world'

'For life is

'You should be dancing, yeah'

quite absurd'

'I'll light the fuse and I'll never lose'

'Waving your banner all over the place'

Boris Johnson
Mayor of London

Jacques Rogge
President of the International
Olympic Committee

Eduardo Paes
Mayor of Rio de Janeiro

Every end has a beginning. As the London 2012
Olympic Games draw to a close, the Olympic
Flag is passed from the Mayor of London to
the President of the IOC, who entrusts it to the
Mayor of Rio de Janeiro – and the search for
2016's heroes begins.

Olympian flame immortal
Whose beacon lights our way
Emblaze our hearts with the fires of hope
On this momentous day

As now we come across the world
To share these Games of old
Let all the flags of every land
In brotherhood unfold

Sing out each nation, voices strong
Rise up in harmony
All hail our brave Olympians
With strains of victory

Olympic light burn on and on
O'er seas and mountains and plains
Unite, inspire, bring honour
To these ascending games

May valour reign victorious
Along the path of golden way

As tomorrow's new champions now come forth
Rising to the fervent spirit of the game
Let splendour pervade each noble deed
Crowned with glory and fame

And let fraternity and fellowship
Surround the soul of every nation

Oh flame, eternal in your firmament so bright
Illuminate us with your everlasting light
That grace and beauty and magnificence

Shine like the sun
Blazing above
Bestow on us your honour, truth and love

Boris Johnson
Maire de Londres

Jacques Rogge
*Président du Comité
International Olympique*

Eduardo Paes
Maire de Rio de Janeiro

*Chaque fin est un début. Alors que les Jeux
Olympiques de Londres 2012 sont sur le point
de s'achever, le maire de Londres va remettre le
drapeau olympique au président du CIO qui le
confiera à son tour au maire de Rio de Janeiro.
Et la quête des héros de 2016 commence...*

*Flamme olympique immortelle
réverbère sur nos chemins
attisez nos coeurs qui brûlent d'espoir
en ce jour de grands exploits*

*Ils s'acheminent de par le monde
jusqu'à ce lieu de rencontre
Chaque étendard de chaque pays
côte à côte en fraternité*

*Le chant des nations fort et fier
résonne en harmonie
Saluons nos braves olympiens
au timbre de la victoire*

*Flamme olympique qui brûle sans cesse
au delà des plaines, des montagnes
et des mers
édifiez-nous de droiture et d'honneur
devant ces nobles jeux*

*Le courage est l'ultime victoire
sur ce chemin qui mène vers l'or*

*Champions de demain fièrement
se présentent souverains
comme le sont ces jeux
Que la splendeur accompagne leurs efforts
couronnés de gloire et de victoire*

*Que la camaraderie et l'éloquence
gouvernent l'esprit de chaque pays*

*Oh flamme olympique
éternelle étoile dans le firmament
éclairez-nous de votre lumière bienfaisante*

*Que la grâce, la beauté, et le courage
brillent comme l'astre qui nous protège
Accordez-nous honneur, vérité, amour*

Embrace

We're extremely proud to receive the Olympic Flag tonight.

The Handover marks the first time a South American country will host the Olympic Games. The Mayor of Rio de Janeiro, Eduardo Paes, will receive the Flag on behalf of over 190 million Brazilians.

The Rio 2016™ Olympic Games will be a memorable celebration, inspiring the planet with our vivacious and happy nature. They'll take place in the world capital of joy, with its youthful spirit and harmonious diversity: Rio de Janeiro, the happiest city of all.

The living, vibrant landscape of Rio reflects the nature of Cariocas and Brazilians, their willingness to welcome all ethnicities, faiths and generations with a warm embrace.

We hope to see you in Rio. Come and join this great feast of passion and transformation, and let the contagious energy of Rio embrace you.

Creative Directors **Cao Hamburger & Daniela Thomas**
Creative Supervisor **Abel Gomes**
Executive Producer **Marco Balich**

'They're lighting up the sky tonight'

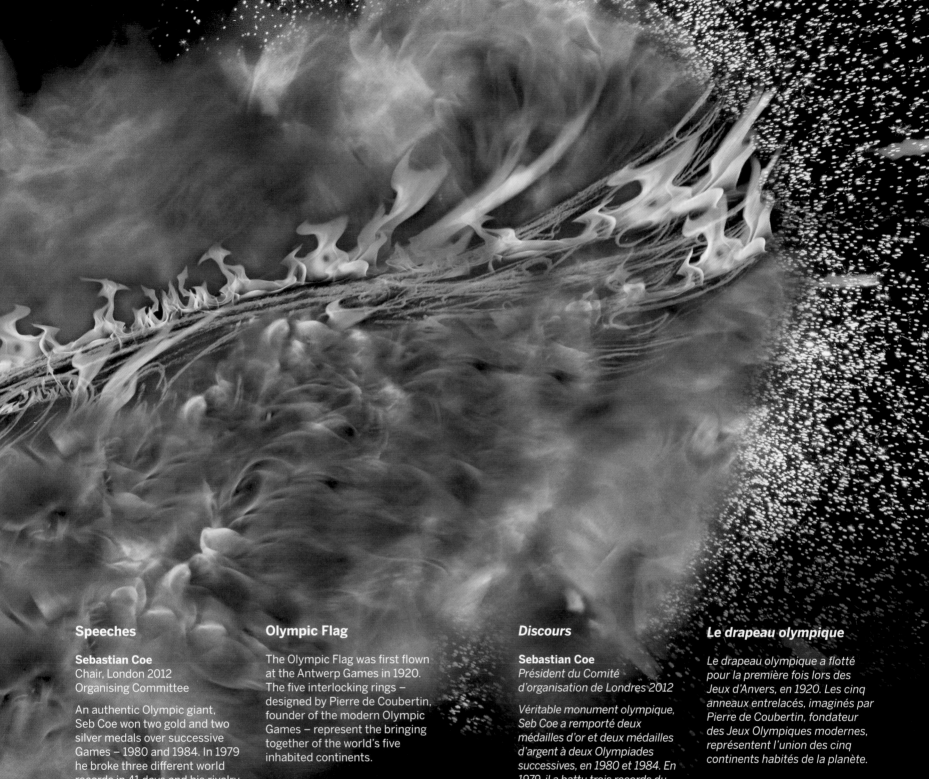

Speeches

Sebastian Coe
Chair, London 2012
Organising Committee

An authentic Olympic giant,
Seb Coe won two gold and two
silver medals over successive
Games – 1980 and 1984. In 1979
he broke three different world
records in 41 days and his rivalry
with fellow middle-distance
runner Steve Ovett is one of the
great Olympic stories.

Jacques Rogge
President of the International
Olympic Committee

Jacques Rogge competed as a
yachtsman over three Olympics
– 1968, 1972 and 1976. This is
his final Games as President
of the IOC, a position he's held
since 2001.

Olympic Flag

The Olympic Flag was first flown
at the Antwerp Games in 1920.
The five interlocking rings –
designed by Pierre de Coubertin,
founder of the modern Olympic
Games – represent the bringing
together of the world's five
inhabited continents.

Spirit of the Flame

Burning bright, noon and night,
across 16 days of sporting
excellence, the Olympic Flame
is now extinguished. A powerful
and poignant moment, it
signifies the end of the London
2012 Olympic Games and the
countdown to Rio 2016.
   But as the final flame flickers
in the Cauldron, a 'Spirit of the
Flame' comes to life above it…

Discours

Sebastian Coe
*Président du Comité
d'organisation de Londres 2012*

*Véritable monument olympique,
Seb Coe a remporté deux
médailles d'or et deux médailles
d'argent à deux Olympiades
successives, en 1980 et 1984. En
1979, il a battu trois records du
monde différents en 41 jours et
sa rivalité avec Steve Ovett, autre
coureur de demi-fond, fait partie
des grandes sagas olympiques.*

Jacques Rogge
*Président du Comité
International Olympique*

*Jacques Rogge a participé aux
épreuves de voile de trois Jeux
Olympiques : 1968, 1972 et 1976.
Ces Jeux sont ses derniers en tant
que président du CIO, poste qu'il*

Le drapeau olympique

*Le drapeau olympique a flotté
pour la première fois lors des
Jeux d'Anvers, en 1920. Les cinq
anneaux entrelacés, imaginés par
Pierre de Coubertin, fondateur
des Jeux Olympiques modernes,
représentent l'union des cinq
continents habités de la planète.*

L'esprit de la Flamme

*Brillant de tout son éclat, jour et
nuit, pendant 16 jours d'excellence
sportive, la Flamme Olympique
va maintenant s'éteindre. C'est
un moment fort et poignant qui
marque la fin des Jeux Olympiques
de Londres 2012 et le début du
compte à rebours pour Rio 2016.
   Mais alors que la dernière
flamme tremble dans la vasque,
un « Esprit de la Flamme » s'élève*

'My Generation': an irreverent hymn
to endless renewal and regeneration.
It's the final song of the Ceremony,
its ultimate manifesto.

My Generation *: un hymne
irrévérencieux à la gloire du
renouveau constant et des
générations à venir. C'est la
chanson finale de la cérémonie,
sa profession de foi.*

'I'm not trying to cause a big s-s-sensation'

'Listening to you, I get the music'

'I'm just talkin' 'bout my g-g-generation'

37

Who's Who?

Qui est qui ?

You'll see thousands of talented performers this evening who've been working with hundreds of creative people behind the scenes to devise and deliver the London 2012 Olympic Games Closing Ceremony.

Vous verrez ce soir des milliers d'artistes de talent qui, en coulisses, ont travaillé avec des centaines de créatifs pour concevoir et vous offrir la cérémonie de clôture des Jeux Olympiques de Londres 2012.

Principal Performers in alphabetical order
Artistes principaux par ordre alphabétique

Alessandra Ambrósio

Alessandra is one of the world's top models. She's the face of large global companies and often appears on the cover of international magazines. She's also an ambassador of NMSS (National Multiple Sclerosis Society) and sponsor of ABEM (Associação Brasileira de Esclerose Múltipla/Brazilian Association for Multiple Sclerosis).

Alessandra est une des mannequins les plus célèbres du monde. Elle est l'image de plusieurs grandes entreprises globales et fait souvent la couverture de magazines internationaux. Elle est aussi ambassadrice de NMSS (National Multiple Sclerosis Society/Société nationale pour la sclérose en plaques) et marraine d'ABEM (Associação Brasileira de Esclerose Múltipla/Association brésilienne pour la sclérose en plaques).

Beady Eye

English rock band Beady Eye was founded in 2009 by former members of Oasis – Liam Gallagher, Gem Archer, Andy Bell and Chris Sharrock. They released their debut album *Different Gear, Still Speeding* in 2011 and have a second album in the pipeline. They've also toured the UK, Europe and America.

Le groupe rock anglais Beady Eye a été fondé en 2009 par Liam Gallagher, Gem Archer, Andy Bell et Chris Sharrock, anciens membres d'Oasis. Leur premier album, Different Gear, Still Speeding, est sorti en 2011 et le deuxième est en cours. Le groupe a aussi fait des tournées au Royaume-Uni, en Europe et en Amérique.

BNegão

BNegão is one of Brazil's most versatile and active rappers. He's performed all over the world, including Japan, USA, Mexico and Europe, and at large festivals such as Roskilde, Eurockéennes and Rock in Rio.

Un des rappeurs les plus actifs et polyvalents du Brésil, BNegão a joué dans le monde entier, y compris au Japon, aux États-Unis, au Mexique et en Europe, ainsi qu'à de grands festivals tels que Roskilde, les Eurockéennes et Rock in Rio.

Russell Brand

Russell's achieved international success as an actor, comedian and writer. He's currently starring in his unscripted, late night series *Brand X* on FX in the USA and has featured in films including *Forgetting Sarah Marshall*, *Arthur* and *Get Him to the Greek*. His autobiography, *My Booky Wook*, was on *The New York Times* bestseller list for five weeks.

Acteur, comique et écrivain, Russell jouit d'un succès international. Il anime son émission d'improvisation Brand X, *actuellement diffusée la nuit aux États-Unis sur FX et a joué dans des films tels que Sans Sarah, rien ne va, Arthur, un amour de milliardaire et American Trip. Son autobiographie,* My Booky Wook, *a figuré sur la liste des best sellers du New York Times pendant cinq semaines.*

Jourdan Dunn

Cool and beautiful international *Vogue* cover girl, Jourdan was the first black model to walk for Prada in 13 years and was a cover star of *Vogue Italia*'s iconic black issue. She's contracted for industry giants Burberry and YSL make-up and is a favourite of designers Dior, Marc Jacobs, Dolce & Gabbana and Louis Vuitton.

Éblouissante et décontractée, Jourdan a fait la couverture de Vogue. Elle a été le premier top model noir à défiler pour Prada en 13 ans et était en couverture du célèbre « numéro noir » du Vogue italien. Elle est sous contrat avec les géants du secteur Burberry et YSL beauté et chère au cœur des créateurs de Dior, Marc Jacobs, Dolce & Gabbana et Louis Vuitton.

Elbow

Over the last five years Elbow have become one of the biggest UK bands in the world. Their multi-platinum album *The Seldom Seen Kid* led to arena tours, a Mercury Music Prize, BRIT and Ivor Novello Awards. The band composed 'First Steps', the BBC's official soundtrack for the London 2012 Olympic Games.

Au cours des cinq dernières années, Elbow est devenu un des plus grands groupes britanniques du monde. Le succès de l'album The Seldom Seen Kid, plusieurs fois disque de platine, a permis au groupe de remplir des stades en tournée et l'a couronné d'un Mercury Music Prize, d'un BRIT Award et d'un Ivor Novello Award. Le groupe a composé First Steps, musique officielle des Jeux Olympiques de Londres 2012 à la BBC.

Karen Elson

International supermodel Karen came to notoriety when she shaved off her eyebrows and dyed her hair bright red for an Italian *Vogue* cover shoot with Steven Meisel. She's since worked for every major fashion brand in the world. Also a singer, she released her debut single 'The Ghost Who Walks' in 2010, produced by Jack White.

Après la couverture de Vogue (Italie), sourcils rasés et cheveux teints en rouge vif devant l'objectif de Steven Meisel, le top model Karen Elson a gagné une réputation internationale. Depuis, elle a travaillé pour toutes les grandes marques de mode du monde. Également chanteuse, elle a sorti son premier titre, The Ghost Who Walks, en 2010, produit par Jack White.

Fatboy Slim

Fatboy Slim was born in Norman Cook's House of Love in Brighton over 15 years ago. In that time he's conquered the world entertaining his adoring fans with his spectacular DJ shows, selling millions of records and making some of the most memorable pop music videos in history.

Fatboy Slim a émergé à la House of Love de Norman Cook à Brighton il y a plus de 15 ans. Au fil de ces années, il a conquis le monde, fascinant ses fans avec de spectaculaires shows de DJ. Il a vendu des millions de disques et ses clips se classent parmi les plus mémorables de l'histoire de la pop.

David Gandy

David has appeared in numerous campaigns and catwalk shows, including Fashion For Relief with Naomi Campbell. He's the face of Dolce & Gabbana's Light Blue fragrance, has worked with top international photographers Mario Testino and Steven Meisel and has appeared on covers of *VMan*, *L'Optimum* and *GQ*.

Visage du parfum Light Blue de Dolce & Gabbana, David a prêté son image à de nombreuses campagnes et a défilé sur de nombreux podiums, y compris pour Fashion for Relief avec Naomi Campbell. Il a travaillé avec des photographes internationaux de renom, tels que Mario Testino et Steven Meisel, et a fait la couverture de VMan, L'Optimum et GQ.

Eric Idle

Eric is a comedian, actor, songwriter and author. He co-created Monty Python, and The Rutles, wrote the worldwide hit, Tony Award-winning musical *Spamalot* (currently in the West End) and the words and music of the classic 'Always Look on the Bright Side of Life'.

Comique, acteur, compositeur et écrivain, Eric est le co-créateur de Monty Python et des Rutles. Il a écrit la comédie musicale mondialement connue Spamalot (actuellement à l'affiche dans le West End) récompensée d'un Tony Award, ainsi que les paroles et la musique du classique Always Look on the Bright Side of Life.

Principal Performers
Artistes principaux

Georgia Jagger

Blessed with the genetic dream team of Jerry Hall and Mick Jagger, Georgia has cultivated her own unique style. She is brand ambassador for Rimmel, Material Girl and has just shot the campaign for her first fragrance. Georgia has appeared in British and American *Vogue*, and continues to work on major international fashion campaigns.

Née du tandem génétique parfait Jerry Hall-Mick Jagger, Georgia a su créer un style bien à elle. Elle est l'ambassadrice des marques Rimmel et Material Girl et vient de tourner la campagne publicitaire de son premier parfum. Georgia a figuré dans Vogue (Royaume-Uni et États-Unis) et travaille pour de grandes campagnes de mode internationales.

Jessie J

Jessie J has hit number one in 19 countries, sold over 2.5 million copies of her debut album, *Who You Are*, and broken UK chart history by becoming the first UK solo artist to achieve six top ten hits from one album. She was recently a coach on BBC talent show, *The Voice*.

Le premier album de Jessie J, Who You Are, *s'est vendu à plus de 2,5 millions d'exemplaires. Jessie J, devenu n°1 dans 19 pays, est aussi le premier artiste solo britannique à avoir six titres du même album classés au top 10 au Royaume-Uni. Elle a aussi été coach à l'émission de la BBC,* The Voice.

Richard Jones

Richard is the bass player with The Feeling, alongside band mates Dan Sells, Ciaran and Kevin Jeremiah and Paul Stewart. They've sold over a million albums, won the Ivor Novello Award for Songwriters of the Year and, in 2006, were the most played act on UK radio.

Richard est bassiste de The Feeling aux côtés de Dan Sells, Ciaran et Kevin Jeremiah et Paul Stewart. Ils ont vendu plus d'un million d'albums, gagné un Ivor Novello Award de meilleurs compositeurs de l'année et furent le groupe le plus diffusé à la radio au Royaume-Uni en 2006.

Seu Jorge

From an early age, Seu knew that he wanted to be a musician. From the age of 10, he attended samba gatherings in Rio de Janeiro, and soon began to sing in night clubs. He describes himself as a popular singer and composer, who likes innumerable musical genres, but whose origins lie in samba.

Seu sait depuis tout jeune qu'il veut être musicien. Dès l'âge de 10 ans, il allait à des rassemblements de samba à Rio de Janeiro et a bientôt commencé à chanter dans des boîtes de nuit. Il se décrit comme étant un chanteur-compositeur populaire aux goûts musicaux très variés mais dont les racines sont la samba.

Kaiser Chiefs

Since the release of their debut chart topping album, *Employment*, in 2005 Kaiser Chiefs have won three BRIT Awards, an Ivor Novello Award and sold over six million albums. As well as touring extensively, they've had four UK top ten albums and six top ten singles including a number one with 'Ruby'.

Depuis la sortie de leur premier album, Employment, *en 2005, propulsé en tête des hit parades, les Kaiser Chiefs ont décroché trois BRIT Awards, un Ivor Novello Award et ont vendu plus de six millions d'albums. En plus de longues tournées, ils ont eu quatre albums et six singles, dont Ruby, classé n° 1, au top 10 britannique.*

Annie Lennox

Singer, songwriter, campaigner and activist, Annie has sold over 80 million records and has been honoured with countless awards for both her music and humanitarian work. Achievements include eight BRIT Awards, four Grammy Awards, an Oscar, a Golden Globe and an OBE in recognition of her tireless campaigning and championing of humanitarian causes.

Chanteuse, auteur de chansons, militante et activiste, Annie a vendu plus de 80 millions de disques et a reçu d'innombrables récompenses tant pour ses talents musicaux que pour son travail humanitaire, notamment huit BRIT Awards, quatre Grammy, un Oscar, un Golden Globe et une décoration de l'Ordre de l'Empire britannique en reconnaissance de son action infatigable en faveur de causes humanitaires.

Julian Lloyd Webber

Acclaimed worldwide as one of the finest cellists of his generation, Julian has worked with an extraordinary array of musicians including Yehudi Menuhin, Georg Solti, Lorin Maazel, Stephane Grappelli, Cleo Laine and Elton John. He plays a rare Stradivarius cello, dating from 1690.

Reconnu dans le monde entier comme un des meilleurs violoncellistes de sa génération, Julian a travaillé avec un éventail de musiciens impressionnant, dont Yehudi Menuhin, Georg Solti, Lorin Maazel, Stéphane Grappelli, Cleo Laine et Elton John. Julian joue sur un violoncelle rare, un stradivarius de 1690.

Madness

Madness are a quintessentially British pop group – nutty, natty and nifty. They've sold more than 10 million albums and had 25 top 40 singles, including 'Baggy Trousers', 'Our House' and 'It Must Be Love'. Their most recent album, *The Liberty of Norton Folgate*, was the most well received of their career.

Madness est le groupe Brit pop par excellence, un petit mélange sympa d'élégance et d'excentricité. Il a vendu plus de 10 millions d'albums, avec 25 singles au top 40, dont Baggy Trousers, Our House *et* It Must Be Love. *Son album le plus récent,* The Liberty of Norton Folgate, *a été le plus apprécié de sa discographie.*

Nick Mason

Nick is the drummer in one of the most creative and enduring bands of all time – Pink Floyd. Over 40 years, Nick has been part of every phase of the band – from London's late 1960s underground, the creation of *The Wall*, world tours in the 90s and the reunion with Roger Waters at Live8 in 2005.

Nick est le batteur de Pink Floyd, un des groupes les plus créatifs et au succès le plus long de l'histoire. Nick a été présent à chaque étape des 40 ans de carrière du groupe, de la période underground londonienne fin des années 60 jusqu'à la réunion du groupe avec Roger Waters pour Live8 en 2005, en passant par la création de The Wall *et les tournées mondiales des années 90.*

George Michael

Over a 30-year career, superstar singer-songwriter George has built a groundbreaking and enormously popular body of work. He's sold over 110 million albums worldwide, topped charts from Austria to Australia, sold out stadiums from Tokyo to Tampa, received numerous international awards and redefined popular music with his number one albums.

En plus de trente ans de carrière, George s'est forgé une réputation planétaire grâce à son œuvre et à ses talents de chanteur et de compositeur. Avec plus de 110 millions d'albums vendus dans le monde, des premières places à tous les hit-parades de l'Autriche à l'Australie, des concerts à guichets fermés de Tokyo à Tampa, il a redéfini la pop et ses albums ont raflé un nombre impressionnant de prix internationaux.

Marisa Monte

Over a 20-year career, Marisa has sold more than 10 million records and won numerous awards. She's recognised as one of the great singers of modern Brazilian music, with a gift for making the connection between traditional music and contemporary pop.

Au long de 20 ans de carrière, Marisa a vendu plus de 10 millions de disques et a reçu de nombreux prix. Elle est reconnue comme une des plus grandes chanteuses de musique brésilienne moderne, douée pour relier musique traditionnelle et pop contemporaine.

Principal Performers
Artistes principaux

Kate Moss

Since being discovered by Storm in 1988, Kate has appeared on the cover of every major international fashion magazine, including 36 covers of British *Vogue*. Recent work includes fronting campaigns for YSL, Dior, Rimmel and Salvatore Ferragamo. Her iconic fashion status has led to design collaborations with Topshop, Longchamp, Fred and Coty.

Découverte par Storm en 1988, Kate a fait la couverture de tous les magazines de mode internationaux, dont 36 fois celle du Vogue britannique. Elle est récemment apparue dans des campagnes YSL, Dior, Rimmel et Salvatore Ferragamo. Son statut d'icône de la mode lui a valu des collaborations créatives avec Topshop, Longchamp, Fred et Coty.

Muse

Since forming in 1994, Muse have released five studio albums, three live albums and an extensive list of top ten singles. Numerous awards include five MTV Europe Music Awards, five *Q* Awards, eight *NME* Awards, two BRIT Awards, four *Kerrang!* Awards, plus a Mercury Prize nomination and three Grammy nominations.

Depuis sa formation en 1994, Muse a sorti cinq albums studio, trois live et une longue liste de singles entrés au top ten. Le groupe a récolté quantité de récompenses : cinq MTV Europe Music Awards, cinq Q Awards, huit NME Awards, deux BRIT Awards, quatre Kerrang! Awards ainsi qu'une nomination au Mercury Prize et trois aux Grammy.

One Direction

Formed two years ago on the UK's *X Factor*, One Direction's debut album, *Up All Night*, has sold over two million copies and hit number one in 16 countries. They became the first British band to reach number one on the US Billboard chart with a debut album and their *Live* DVD has been number one in 27 countries.

Ce groupe a été fondé il y a deux ans lors d'une participation au X Factor britannique. Up All Night, le premier album de One Direction, s'est vendu à plus de deux millions d'exemplaires et s'est hissé au sommet des classements dans 16 pays. C'est le premier groupe britannique en tête des hit-parades américains avec son premier album. Leur DVD Live a été n° 1 dans 27 pays.

Pet Shop Boys

After seven UK platinum albums, collaborations with Dusty Springfield, David Bowie and Liza Minnelli, a ballet for Sadler's Wells and a score for *Battleship Potemkin*, the duo were presented with the Outstanding Contribution to Music Award at the BRIT Awards in 2009. Their new studio album, *Elysium*, is released later this year.

Avec à son actif sept disques de platine britanniques, des collaborations avec Dusty Springfield, David Bowie et Liza Minnelli, un ballet créé pour Sadler's Wells et un accompagnement musical pour Le Cuirassé Potemkine, ce duo a en outre reçu un BRIT Award pour Contribution Exceptionnelle à la Musique en 2009. Leur nouvel album studio, Elysium, est attendu cette année.

Queen

Rock legends Queen are responsible for some of the best-known songs in the world, including stadium anthems 'We Will Rock You' and 'We Are the Champions'. Their *Greatest Hits* album is Britain's bestselling album ever and their single 'Bohemian Rhapsody' is year-on-year voted the best single of all time.

Le groupe Queen est une légende du rock : il a signé quelques-uns des airs les plus célèbres du monde, dont les classiques des stades, We Will Rock You et We Are the Champions. Greatest Hits reste l'album le plus vendu de l'histoire en Grande-Bretagne et Bohemian Rhapsody est réélu "meilleur single de tous les temps" année après année.

Mike Rutherford

Mike is a founder member, guitarist, bassist and songwriter with Genesis. Over four decades the band has sold over 150 million albums and played more than 4,000 live shows. In 1984 he formed Mike & The Mechanics and had a succession of international hits, including 'The Living Years'.

Mike est un des membres fondateur, guitariste, bassiste et auteur-compositeur de Genesis. Depuis plus de quatre décennies, le groupe a vendu plus de 150 millions d'albums et a joué plus de 4 000 spectacles. En 1984, il a formé Mike & The Mechanics et a connu une succession de hits internationaux, y compris « The Living Years ».

Emeli Sandé

BRIT Awards Critics' Choice winner Emeli has written songs for some of the biggest names in pop. Revered by her peers and championed by artists like Alicia Keys and Coldplay's Chris Martin, she released her debut album *Our Version of Events* in 2012 which reached number one in the charts.

Emeli, lauréate du prix Choix de la Critique des BRIT Awards, a composé des morceaux pour les plus grands noms de la pop : très estimée par le reste de la profession, elle a été mise en avant par Alicia Keys et Chris Martin de Coldplay. Our Version of Events, son premier album, s'est classé en tête des hit-parades en 2012.

Ed Sheeran

Ed's debut album + sold more than 100,000 copies in its first week, making it the biggest selling debut for a UK male in over 10 years. He's racked up a myriad of accolades, including two BRIT Awards, and has played at major UK festivals as well as selling out all of his headline shows.

Le premier album d'Ed, +, s'est vendu à plus de 100 000 exemplaires dans la semaine suivant sa sortie, ce qui en fait le meilleur début d'un album masculin britannique depuis 10 ans. Ed a collecté une ribambelle de récompenses, dont deux BRIT Awards, a joué à de grands festivals du Royaume-Uni et devant des salles combles à tous ses concerts de tête d'affiche.

Renato Sorriso

Renato found fame in 1997 when, instead of sweeping the track of the Sambodrome, he started to dance. The public loved his samba skills and charisma, which has made him popular with the Brazilian media and in demand on the lecture circuit.

La gloire de Renato a démarré en 1997 quand, au lieu de simplement défiler au Sambodrome, il s'est mis à danser. La foule ayant adoré son talent et son charisme, les médias brésiliens lui prêtent beaucoup d'attention et les tournées de conférences se l'arrachent.

Principal Performers
Artistes principaux

Timothy Spall

One of Britain's most talented character actors, Timothy has had a distinguished career on stage and screen. Recent work includes playing Peter Pettigrew in the Harry Potter films, Winston Churchill in *The King's Speech*, Peter Taylor in *The Damned United* and the BAFTA-nominated documentary *Timothy Spall: Back at Sea*.

Timothy Spall est un des acteurs de genre britanniques les plus talentueux. Sa carrière embrasse la scène et le cinéma. Il a récemment joué Peter Pettigrew dans les Harry Potter, Churchill dans Le discours d'un roi ou encore Peter Taylor dans The Damned United. Le documentaire Timothy Spall: Back at Sea a été nominé aux BAFTA.

The Spice Girls

The Spice Girls are the biggest-selling girl group of all time, selling over 75 million records. Their debut album Spice sold more than 28 million copies worldwide, they've had nine UK number one singles and 'Wannabe' is the biggest-selling single ever by an all-female group, reaching number one in more than 30 countries.

Avec des ventes à hauteur de 75 millions, les Spice Girls sont le groupe féminin qui a vendu le plus de disques de l'histoire. Leur premier album, Spice, s'est vendu à plus de 28 millions d'exemplaires dans le monde, neuf de leurs singles se sont classés numéro un en Grande-Bretagne et Wannabe est le titre féminin qui détient le record des ventes, avec une première place dans plus de 30 pays.

Take That

Since forming in 1990, Take That have had 54 number one singles and 35 number one albums around the world, winning a string of awards along the way. *Progress* (2010) is the second fastest selling album in British history, while Progress Live (2011) was the fastest selling UK tour of all time.

Depuis sa formation en 1990, Take That s'est adjugé 54 meilleures ventes de singles, 35 albums n° 1 à l'échelle mondiale et toute une série de prix. Progress (2010) est le deuxième album à s'être vendu le plus vite de l'histoire du Royaume-Uni tandis que la tournée Progress Live (en 2011) s'est également vendue à une vitesse record.

Tinie Tempah

Since releasing his debut number one single 'Pass Out' in 2010, Tinie Tempah has picked up two BRIT Awards, three MOBOs, an Ivor Novello Award, achieved double-platinum with his album, *Disc-Overy*, and sold out a UK arena tour. Known for his unique style, he's also launched a clothing line, Disturbing London.

Depuis le lancement de son premier single Pass Out *en 2010, Tinie Tempah a décroché deux BRIT Awards, trois MOBO, un Ivor Novello et obtenu un double disque de platine pour l'album* Disc-Overy. *Sa tournée britannique a affiché complet. Connu pour son style unique, il a également lancé Disturbing London, une ligne de vêtements.*

Stella Tennant

Granddaughter of the Duke of Devonshire, Stella's potential as a model was spotted by iconic photographer Steven Meisel. She appeared in a range of campaigns before becoming the face of Chanel and muse to Karl Lagerfeld in 1996. She remains a prominent force in the fashion industry. Recent campaigns include Givenchy, Balenciaga and Celine.

Stella est la petite-fille du duc de Devonshire. Son potentiel en tant que mannequin a été repéré par le grand photographe de mode Steven Meisel. Elle a figuré dans plusieurs campagnes avant de devenir le visage de Chanel et la muse de Karl Lagerfeld en 1996. Elle reste une force de premier plan dans le monde de la mode et a récemment participé aux campagnes Givenchy, Balenciaga et Céline.

The Who

The genius of Pete Townshend's songwriting and guitar playing and Roger Daltrey's vocals continue as The Who reach the end of their fifth decade, despite the loss of original members Keith Moon and John Entwistle. With 100m albums sold, numerous awards and millions raised for charity, their Olympic appearance is one of many major events – from Woodstock to Live Aid, the 2001 Concert for New York and the Super Bowl.

Le génie du compositeur et guitariste Pete Townshend et du chanteur Roger Daltrey continue à briller alors que The Who est sur le point de fêter son cinquantenaire en dépit de la disparition de Keith Moon et de John Entwistle. Après cent millions d'albums vendus, une ribambelle de récompenses, des sommes importantes récoltées pour les bonnes causes, les Jeux s'ajoutent à la liste d'évènements majeurs auxquels ils ont participé : de Woodstock à Live Aid, du Concert for New York de 2001 au Super Bowl.

Performers
Artistes

Stadium Announcers
Trish Bertram
Marc Edwards

Pre-Show

Pre-Show Host
Andy Collins

Band Leader
Joe Dieffenbacher

Stomp
Dan Baines
Phil Batchelor
Ignazio Bellini
Paul Bend
Johannes Bohun
Adam Buckley
Omari Carter
Nigel Clarke
Simone Clarke
Nathaniel Conroy
Pedro Consorte
Hugo Cortes
Luke Cresswell
Aideen Gallagher
Paul Gunter
William Hickling
Melanie Joseph
Michael Landis
James Lane
Sarah Lasaki
Laetitia Lawrence
Jasper Little
Guido Mandozzi
Melone M'Kenzy
Serena Morgan
Fraser Morrison
Cameron Newlin
Peter Nielsen
Sune Nielsen
Arild Nyborg
Fred Nye
Andrew Patrick
Leela Petronio Mourrat
Paul Russell
Gemma Shields
Reggie Talley
Ian Vincent
Simeon Weedall
Joe White
Paul White

Rush Hour

Dance Captains
Sarah-Jane Aboboto
Briony Albert
Lucy Banfield
Teneisha Bonner
Ben Campbell
Jennifer Chapman
Ciaran Connolly
Gareth Davis
Layla Ellison
Adrian Gas
Lizzie Gough
Jared Hageman
Nathan Holliday
Mandy Liddell
Claire Millin
Douglas Mills
Susan Shaw
Aaron Sillis

Felicity Todd
Jackson Williams

Dancers
Kamilah Afiyah-Beckles
Cem Ahmet
Curtis Angus
Luke Bartholomew
Amii Bell
Stephanie Billers
Charlie Bruce
Becky Butler
Simon Campbell
Shaun Capewell
Michelle Carter
Cherie Cheung
Kelly Chow
Callum Clack
Scott Michael Coldwell
Stephanie Collins
Dan Cooke
Tom Cunningham
Keely Dann
Emma De Vees
Charlene Dinger
Helen Dixon
Nyroy Dixon
Michael Downing
Ella Durston
Erin Dusek
Martin Fenton
Luke Field-Wright
Majella Fitzgerald
Nicholas Gilligan
Tom Goodall
Zoe Green
Leanne Hainsby
Andrew Hamshire
Crystal Rose Hantig
Becky Hicks
Harry Hodges
Andrea Howarth
Alex Jackson
David Jamerson
Oliver John John
Dan Keightley
Adam-Marc Kelly
Kate Kelly
Samir Khan
Gemma Kneale
Gemma Lawrence
Del Mak
Alec Mann
Kevin McGuire
Tobias Mead
Oliver Metzler
Mandy Montanez
Shiloh Nelson
David Page
Chris Piper
Rachel Quartley
James Rees
Rohan Richards
Amber Rimmell
James Robinson
Sarah Robinson
Brett Rosengreen
Laura Rylands
Ross Sands
Paul Saunders
Craig Scott
Tom Shilcock
Nathalie Smith
Pamela Smith
Lorraine Stewart
Matt Sussman
Jasmine Takacs

Samantha Tan
Senay Taormina
Bethany Rose Teagle
Alice Walker
Laura Walker
Oliver Wheeler
Johnny White
Sean Williams
Jay Wilson

Drivers
Matt Deeley
Kate Fernandez
Thomas Ford
Nick Hugh
Cameron Jack
Ben Jeffery
Toby Jeffery
James Mabbett
Vicky Macpherson
Karen McAllister
Josh McKay
Tony Readdie
Gareth Richman
Martin Unsby

God Save the Queen

Flag Team Leader
**Squadron Leader Pullen,
Royal Air Force, RAF
Abbeywood**

Flag Bearers
**Lance Sergeant Hay, Army,
Unit F Company Scots Guards**
**Captain Mills, Royal Marines,
Royal Marines Reserve City
of London**
**Sergeant Odell, Royal Air
Force, RAF Lyneham**
**Corporal of the Horse
Puddifoot, Army, Household
Cavalry Mounted Regiment**
**Warrant Officer Class 1
Randle, Royal Navy, HMS
Raleigh**
**Leading Steward Robertson,
Royal Navy, HMS
Northumberland**
**Squadron Leader Smith,
Royal Air Force, RAF High
Wycombe**

Flag Raisers
**Guardsman Attuguayefio,
Army, Wellington Barracks**
**Corporal Gerrard, Royal
Marines, North Devon**
**Flight Sergeant Tate, Royal
Air Force, RAF Henlow**

Street Party

Del Boy
Anthony Renshaw

Rodney
Christopher Unwin

Waterloo Sunset

Acrobats
Erick Adame
Remy Archer
Jack Atherton
James Booth
Ben Brason
Bowen Cang
Jono Fee
Chris Gage
Jack Helme
James Higgins
Jack Horner
Steve Hough
Steven Jehu
Conor Kenny
Terry Lamb
Dan Lanningan
Adam Laughton
Rachael Letsche
Zeming Lian
Christer Pettersen
David Rimmer
Samantha Rockett
Hasit Savani
Olga Simet
Ahmahd Thomas
Veliko Velikov
Kylie Walker
Jianbo Wang
Anthony Weiss
Kristof Willerton
Steve Williams
Hadyn Wiseman
Davd-Roy Wood

Here Comes the Sun

The Dhol Foundation Drummers
Gurpal Bhachu
Pritpal Bharaj
Steven Cheema
Harjit Dev
Suraj Gill
Arjun Johal
Harry Kalsi
Jo Kalsi
Johnny Kalsi
Simon Pal
Vinesh Patel
Onkar Phull
Amandeep Rallh
Satnam Rooprai
Ravinder Sandhu
Ritu Sharma
Arun Singh Cheema

A Symphony of British Music

Always Look on the Bright Side
Opera Singer
Susan Bullock

The Company Drummers
Danielle Bancroft
Sofia Bancroft
Robin Barraclough
Carly Bourne
Joel Brogan
Ian Butt
John Calvert
Andrew Cartwright
Richard Cartwright

Bryn Cattell
Grant Cattell
Gemma Clarke
Adam Croft
Christian Daly
Matthew Daly
Rebekka Evans
Dino Franchi
Nicholas Hankin
Phillip Hargreaves
Timothy Harper
Gillian Harrison
Luke Hawley
Claire Hein
Rebecca Hein
Nigel Jackson
Thomas Jepson
Stephanie Kaye
Georgia Kilshaw
Mark Long
Samuel Manger
Georgia Moran
Gregory Newbold
Lee Nuttall
Darren O'Meara
Nathan Parker
Christopher Powell
Matthew Powell
Heather Rotchell
Thomas Shepherd
John Stovin
Wayne Sunderland
Maria Tarrant
Kirsty White
Lee Whitehead
Alice Whiteley
Jack Whiteley
Sally Whiteley
Christopher Wilmott
Jordan Wright-Murray

High Wire Artist
Laszlo Simet

Wish You Were Here
Businessmen
James Cohen
Dapo Coker
Kieran Daley-Ward
Ramon Diaz Crosdale
Edward Hayes-Neary
Shem Jacobs
Gavin Johnson Assoon
Jamie Karitzis
Ossian Luke
Alexander Murdoch
Wolfgang Mwanje
Darron Opoku-Abebreseh
Victor Osborne
Antony Palmer
Joel Palmer
Steve Richardson
James Robinson
Mark Andrew Robson
Alex Thomas
Anthony Trahearn
Stephen Walker
Kevin Young
Nicholas Zabilowicz

Angels with Wings
Anya Barker
Agathe Chapman De Lussy
Sharmina Harrower
Lisa Omand
Penelope Simpson
Amabel Torrance

Miroslava Vaclavova
Florence Whittaker
Megan Williams

Bond String Quartet
Eos Chater
Tania Lee Davis
Elspeth Hanson
Gay-Yee Westerhoff

Cannon Men
Chachi Valencia
Robin Lynn Valencia

Nuns on Skates
Charmaine Ashmore
Hazel Duckworth
Frankie Poultney
Corinna Stewart
Simone Thornett
Philippa Towler-Green
Leigh Walker
Deborah Young

Formation Taxi Drivers
Phil Ellis
Tommy Erdos
Phil Keen
Darren Malkin
James Rhodes

Fashion Quad Bike Riders
Andrew Bentley
Charlie Butler-Henderson
Andre D'Cruze
James Littlejohn
Tim Marshall
Will Schryver
Jack Stanford
Jamie Wall

Pinball Wizard Vespa Rider
Matt Sherren

Flying Machine People
Eric Adame
Remy Archer
Abagail Evans
Ted Siktröm

The Road to Rio

Flag Team Leader
Flag Bearers
Flag Raisers
(See God Save the Queen)

Flag Lowerers
**Medicine Marine Moynihan,
Royal Marines, Plymouth**
**Squadron Leader Stagles,
Royal Air Force, Birmingham
Royal Centre for Defence
Leading Physical Training
Instructor Jackson, Royal
Navy, HMS Drake**

Spirit of the Flame

Ballet Principals
Gary Avis
Jonathan Cope
Nehemiah Kish
Ed Watson

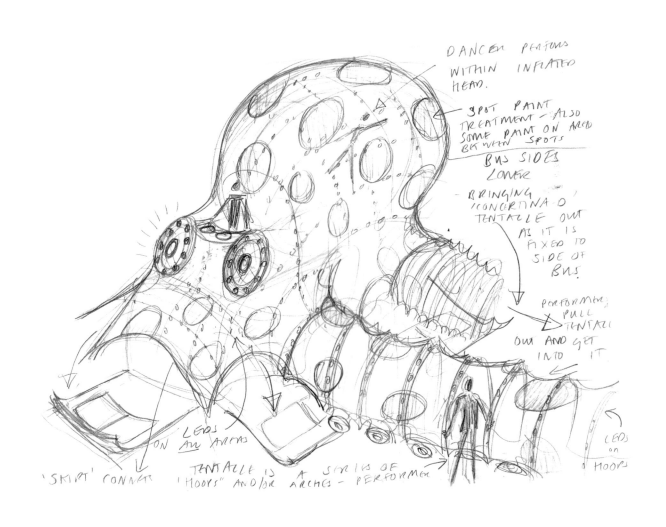

DANCER PERFORMS WITHIN INFLATED HEAD.

SPOT PAINT TREATMENT - ALSO SOME PAINT ON AREA BETWEEN SPOTS

BUS SIDES LOWER

BRINGING CONCERTINA-O TENTACLE OUT AS IT IS FIXED TO SIDE OF BUS.

PERFORMERS PULL TENTACLE OUT AND GET INTO IT

LEDS ON ARMS

LEDS ON HOOPS

'SKIRT' CONNECT

TENTACLE IS A SERIES OF 'HOOPS' AND/OR ARCHES - PERFORMER

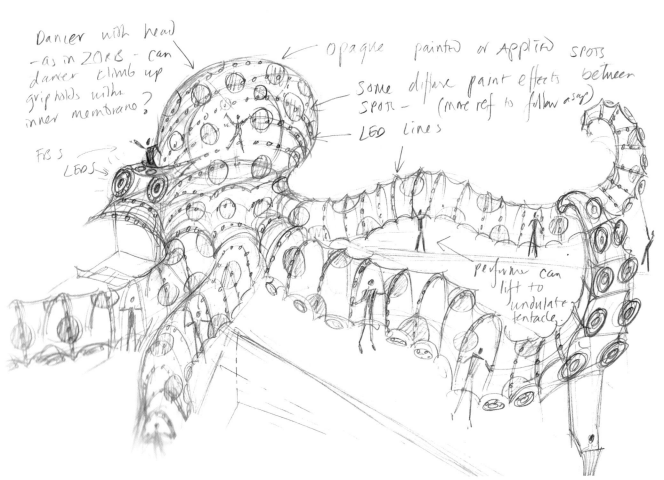

Dancer with head - as in ZORB - can dancer climb up gripholds with inner membrane?

Opaque painted or APPLIED SPOTS

Some diffuse paint effects between SPOTS - (more ref to follow asap)

LED lines

FIBS LEDS

Performer can lift to undulate tentacle.

Executive Team
Équipe exécutive

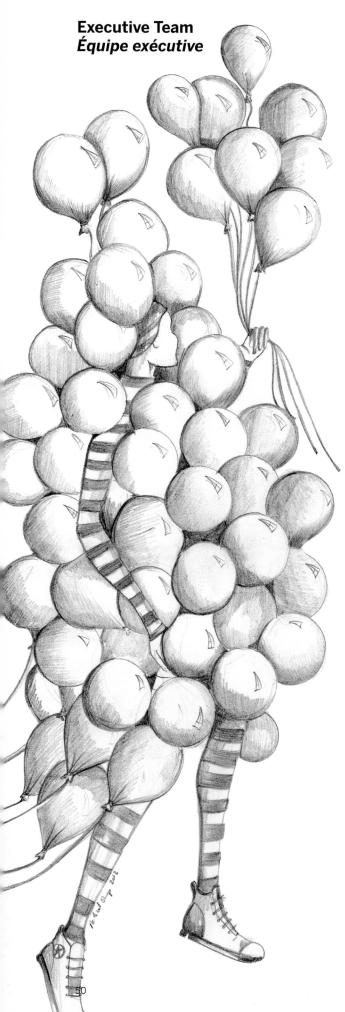

Bill Morris
Director of Ceremonies,
Education & Live Sites

Bill joined London 2012 six years ago from the BBC where he started as a journalist, moved into radio and TV production and executive roles, before specialising in major events as Project Director Live Events. These included the BBC Music Live festival, the annual BBC Proms in the Park, the Olympic Torch Relay Concert in London's Mall, and the Queen's Concerts at Buckingham Palace (for which he was awarded the LVO in the Queen's Jubilee Honours List). He also coordinated broadcast live events across a number of BBC radio and television services, including Live 8 in 2005. Bill served on the Radio Academy's Council from the early 1990s, he was Chair 1998-2001, and was made a Fellow in 2001.

Avant de rejoindre Londres 2012 il y a six ans, Bill était à la BBC, où il a commencé comme journaliste puis a travaillé à la production radio et télévision et assumé des fonctions de direction. Il s'est ensuite spécialisé dans les grands événements, devenant directeur de projets sur les événements live comme le festival BBC Music Live, la manifestation annuelle BBC Proms in the Park, le concert du relais de la flamme olympique au London's Mall et les Queen's Concerts à Buckingham Palace (pour lesquels il a été fait Lieutenant de l'ordre royal de Victoria à l'occasion de la promotion du Jubilé de la Reine). Il a aussi coordonné plusieurs événements en direct diffusés sur les services de radio et de télévision de la BBC, dont la série de concerts Live 8, en 2005. Bill a intégré le conseil de la Radio Academy au début des années 90 et en a été président de 1998 à 2001. Il en est devenu membre associé (Fellow) en 2001.

Martin Green
Head of Ceremonies

Trained in writing and directing theatre, Martin spent five years as Head of Events for the Mayor of London where he was responsible for producing global events such as the London New Year's Eve fireworks, major music festivals and one-off events across the city. As Director of Events at the O2 he oversaw the reopening of this now hugely successful venue. He joined London 2012 in 2007 as Head of Ceremonies, where he has recruited and inspired a world class team to deliver the Torch Relays, Victory Ceremonies, Team Welcome Ceremonies, and Opening and Closing Ceremonies of the Olympic and Paralympic Games.

Formé à l'écriture et la mise en scène théâtrale, Martin a été pendant cinq ans responsable événementiel pour le maire de Londres, poste où il avait en charge la production d'événements globaux tels que les feux d'artifice du 31 décembre à Londres, les grands festivals musicaux et les événements ponctuels organisés au sein de la ville. En tant que directeur événementiel de l'O2, il a supervisé la réouverture de ce site qui rencontre aujourd'hui un immense succès. Il a rejoint Londres 2012 en 2007 en tant que responsable des cérémonies, poste où il a recruté et inspiré une équipe de tout premier plan pour organiser les relais de la flamme, les cérémonies des vainqueurs, les cérémonies d'accueil des équipes ainsi que les cérémonies d'ouverture et de clôture des Jeux Olympiques et Paralympiques.

Catherine Ugwu
Executive Producer, Production

Catherine is a creative director, executive producer and consultant and has been involved in some of the world's largest and most prestigious public events. She was Executive Producer for the Glasgow Handover Ceremony of the Delhi 2010 Commonwealth Games; Senior Producer for the strategic phase of the Opening, Closing and Victory Ceremonies of the 2010 Vancouver Winter Olympics; she produced the Opening Ceremony for the Asian Games in Doha, Qatar in 2006, the Closing Ceremony for the Commonwealth Games in Manchester in 2002 and a large-scale performance spectacle to mark the opening of the Millennium Dome, London in 2000.

Directrice de la création, productrice exécutive et consultante, Catherine a contribué à certains des événements publics les plus importants et les plus prestigieux au monde. Productrice exécutive pour la cérémonie de passage à Glasgow des Jeux du Commonwealth de 2010 à Delhi, elle a été productrice sénior pour la phase stratégique des cérémonies d'ouverture, de clôture et des vainqueurs des Jeux Olympiques d'hiver de 2010 à Vancouver. Elle a également produit la cérémonie d'ouverture des Jeux asiatiques de Doha, au Qatar, en 2006, ainsi que la cérémonie de clôture des Jeux du Commonwealth à Manchester en 2002 et un spectacle de grande envergure pour marquer l'ouverture du Dôme du millénaire, à Londres, en 2000.

Stephen Daldry
Executive Producer, Creative

Stephen started his career at Sheffield's Crucible Theatre and directed extensively in Britain's regional theatres. In London he was Artistic Director of the Gate and Royal Court theatres; he's directed at the National Theatre, the Public Theatre in New York and transferred many productions to the West End and Broadway. His production of *Billy Elliot: The Musical* is currently playing in London and on tour in the USA. It recently won more Tony Awards (10) than any other British show in Broadway history. He's also made four films: *Billy Elliot*; *The Hours*; *The Reader*; and *Extremely Loud & Incredibly Close*.

Stephen a commencé sa carrière au Crucible Theatre de Sheffield et a mis en scène de nombreuses pièces dans les théâtres régionaux britanniques. À Londres, il a été directeur artistique du Gate Theatre et du Royal Court Theatre. Il a également mis en scène des pièces au National Theatre et au Public Theatre de New York et a transposé de nombreuses productions dans le West End et à Broadway. Sa production Billy Elliot: The Musical est actuellement à l'affiche à Londres et en tournée aux États-Unis. Elle a récemment remporté plus de Tony Awards (dix) que n'en a jamais reçu un autre spectacle britannique à Broadway. Stephen a également réalisé quatre films : Billy Elliot, The Hours, The Reader et Extrêmement fort et incroyablement près.

Hamish Hamilton
Executive Producer, Broadcast/TV

Hamish, from Blackpool, is a Grammy nominated, multi-camera television and video director. He began his career as a trainee with BBC Scotland and as a TV director for the BBC Manchester Youth Programmes Unit. Pursuing his love of live music, he's directed the BRIT Awards, the MTV European Music Awards and the Victoria's Secret Fashion Shows for nine years. His credit appears on nearly 30 million live concert DVDs. His most recent work includes the Oscars, the MTV Video Music Awards and the Super Bowl halftime shows. He is also Creative Director of the television and event production company, Done and Dusted.

Originaire de Blackpool, Hamish est un réalisateur de télévision et de vidéos multicaméras nominé aux Grammy Awards. Après avoir débuté comme stagiaire à la BBC Écosse puis réalisateur TV pour l'Unité de programmes jeunesse de la BBC Manchester, son amour de la musique en direct l'a amené à réaliser les BRIT Awards, les MTV European Music Awards et les défilés de mode de la marque Victoria's Secret pendant neuf ans. Son nom apparaît au générique de près de 30 millions de DVD de concerts en direct. Ses réalisations les plus récentes concernent notamment les Oscars, les MTV Video Music Awards et les spectacles de la mi-temps au Super Bowl. Il est également directeur de la création de la société de production télévisée et événementielle Done and Dusted.

Mark Fisher
Executive Producer, Design

Mark's show design credits include *The Wall* for Pink Floyd in 1980 and Roger Waters in 2010; every Rolling Stones show since 1989 and every U2 concert since 1992. His architecturally innovative outdoor stages have been constructed several thousand times in cities all over the world. His event design credits include the Opening and Closing Ceremonies for the 2010 Commonwealth Games in Delhi, the 2010 Asian Games in Guangzhou and the 2008 Beijing Olympic Games. His theatre shows include *KÀ* and *Viva Elvis* for Cirque du Soleil in Las Vegas.

Mark a signé la conception scénique de The Wall *pour Pink Floyd en 1980 et Roger Waters en 2010, tous les spectacles des Rolling Stones depuis 1989 et tous les concerts de U2 depuis 1992. Ses scènes d'extérieur à l'architecture novatrice ont été montées des milliers de fois dans des villes du monde entier. En matière d'événementiel, il a conçu les cérémonies d'ouverture et de clôture des Jeux du Commonwealth de Delhi en 2010, des Jeux Asiatiques de Canton en 2010 et des Jeux Olympiques de Pékin en 2008. Au théâtre, il a conçu les spectacles KÀ et Viva Elvis pour Le Cirque du Soleil à Las Vegas.*

Artistic Team
Équipe artistique

Kim Gavin
Artistic Director

Kim is widely recognised as one of the UK's leading creative directors and choreographers. From one-off TV specials to record-breaking stadium shows, he's been the creative vision behind some of the most innovative and inspirational performances in the world of music and live events over the last 18 years. Kim trained at the Royal Ballet School and after a successful career as a dancer he turned towards choreography, stage and creative direction. Recent credits include Take That's critically acclaimed Circus and Progress Tours, Children in Need Rocks, and many individual artists' performances at the BRIT Awards and Royal Variety Performance.

Kim est reconnu comme un des directeurs artistiques et chorégraphes britanniques de premier plan. Des projets télévisés exceptionnels aux grands spectacles dans les stades, il a été, ces 18 dernières années, l'éminence créative des manifestations les plus innovantes et passionnantes dans le monde du spectacle et de la musique. Kim a étudié à la Royal Ballet School et après une belle carrière de danseur, il s'est tourné vers la chorégraphie, la mise en scène et la direction artistique. Il a récemment été en charge des tournées Circus et Progress de Take That, de Children in Need Rocks et des mises en scène d'artistes individuels aux BRIT Awards et à la Royal Variety Performance.

Nathan Clarke
Associate Director

Nathan trained as a dancer in Australia and performed worldwide before moving into choreography. Choreography credits include Burlesque (Germany and France), The Overtones, Bananarama, JLS and, as Assistant Choreographer to Kim Gavin, Take That, Katherine Jenkins and Viva La Diva tours, The BRIT Awards and Royal Variety Performances.

Nathan a étudié comme danseur en Australie et s'est produit partout dans le monde avant de s'intéresser à la chorégraphie. On compte à son actif Burlesque (France et Allemagne), The Overtones, Bananarama et JLS. Il a également collaboré avec Kim Gavin sur la chorégraphie pour Take That, Katherine Jenkins et Viva La Diva, les BRIT Awards et la Royal Variety Performance.

Gareth Walker
Associate Director

Gareth's credits include creative director/choreography for Steps, Anastasia, Lulu, Chaka Khan and Mika; choreography for the Royal Variety Performance and the BRIT Awards; assistant choreography for Take That's Ultimate, Beautiful World and Circus tours; and show director for L'Oreal, Toyota and GHD. He's also presented and choreographed Ministry of Sound's fitness DVDs.

Gareth a été directeur artistique-chorégraphe pour Steps, Anastasia, Lulu, Chaka Khan et Mika. Il était responsable de la chorégraphie pour les BRIT Awards et la Royal Variety Performance ainsi qu'assistant-chorégraphe pour les tournées Ultimate, Beautiful World et Circus de Take That. Enfin, il a assuré la direction artistique de manifestations pour L'Oreal, Toyota et GHD. Il a aussi animé et chorégraphié le DVD de fitness du Ministry of Sound.

David Arnold
Music Director

David is a Grammy, BAFTA, Ivor Novello and RTS award-winning composer, songwriter and producer. Film scores include *Independence Day*, *Zoolander*, *Hot Fuzz* and five James Bond movies. He also works in theatre and television (*Sherlock*, *Little Britain*) and writes and produces with artists as diverse as Iggy Pop, KD Lang and George Michael.

David est auteur-compositeur et producteur, lauréat des Grammy, BAFTA, Ivor Novello et RTS Awards. Il a signé la musique de films comme Independence Day, Zoolander, Hot Fuzz et cinq James Bond. Il travaille également pour la scène et la télévision (Sherlock, Little Britain). Enfin, il compose et collabore à la production pour des artistes aussi divers qu'Iggy Pop, KD Lang et George Michael.

Es Devlin
Designer

Es' designs include opera (Royal Opera House, ENO, La Scala), drama (RSC, National Theatre, Complicite) dance (Sadler's Wells, Rambert) and pop concerts (Take That, Lady Gaga, Kanye West). Recent awards include TPi Stage Designer of the Year 2010, 2011 and 2012, *Red*'s Creative Woman of the Year 2011 and Olivier Award 2006.

Es a travaillé pour l'opéra (Royal Opera House, ENO, La Scala), le théâtre (RSC, National Theatre, Complicite), la danse (Sadler's Wells, Rambert) et des concerts pop (Take That, Lady Gaga, Kanye West). Elle a reçu le prix du créateur de scène du TPi en 2010, 2011 et 2012 et le prix Olivier en 2006 et a en outre été élue Femme Créative de l'année 2011 par le magazine Red.

Michael Sharp
Costume Designer

Michael has designed shows and costumes for high profile productions, music tours and videos worldwide. Working from studios in England and France, his credits include Take That's Ultimate, Beautiful World, Progress and Circus tours, Darcey Bussell, Katherine Jenkins, Goldfrapp and the BRIT Awards.

Michael a conçu des spectacles et costumes pour des productions, des tournées musicales et des clips de premier plan partout dans le monde. Il travaille dans ses studios en France et au Royaume-Uni, notamment sur les tournées Beautiful World, Progress et Circus de Take That, ainsi que sur des spectacles de Darcey Bussell, Katherine Jenkins, Goldfrapp et sur les BRIT Awards.

Debbie Phillips
Producer

Debbie has produced and executive produced some of the biggest live music events around the globe. Highlights include producing the MTV Europe Music Awards for over seven years, live concerts with the biggest international acts, and non-music based events such as the Laureus World Sports Awards and Nickelodeon Kids' Choice Awards.

Debbie a été productrice et productrice déléguée sur certains des plus grands évènements musicaux du monde, notamment productrice de la cérémonie des MTV Europe Music Awards pendant plus de sept ans, des concerts des plus grandes stars internationales ainsi que d'évènements non musicaux comme les Laureus World Sports Awards ou les Nickelodeon Kids' Choice Awards.

Production Team: Creative
Équipe de production créative

Aerial & Special Skills

Phil Hayes Aerial & Special Skills Consultant
Alex Poulter Aerial & Special Skills Associate

Audio Visual & Broadcast

Ballet Choreography

Alistair Marriott,
Christopher Wheeldon Choreographers
Jackie Barrett, Jonathan Howells,
Cindy Jourdain Assistant Choreographers

Justine Catterall Head of Audio Visual
Adam Dadswell Presentation Manager
David Watson Digital Media Manager
Lizzie Pocock Audio Visual Department Coordinator
Charlotte Andrews AV Production Assistant

Steven Harris Video Documentation
Graham Carlow Photographer
Matt Askem Video Screens Director
Tracey Askem Video Screens Production Assistant
Jane Jackson Broadcast Liaison Manager

Casting

Gillian Schofield Cast Manager,
Professional
Sarah Chambers, Jane Salberg
Cast Coordinators, Professional
Penny Davies Cast Coordinator,
Professional & Volunteers
Rhian Davies Assistant Cast
Coordinator, Professional
Sarah Murray Casting Assistant,
Professional
Nichola Bouchard Company Manager

Sara-Ellen Williams Cast Manager,
Volunteers
Sara Berutto, Maz Bryden, Dianne Leach,
Trish McClenaghan, Laura Windows
Senior Cast Coordinators, Volunteers
Barbara Lisicki Access Manager
Michael Foley, Glenda Genovesi,
Vanessa Griffiths, Helen Lam,
Haitham Ridha Cast Coordinators,
Volunteers
Jenny Rogers Cast Coordinator, Schools
Cheryl Galbraith, Martin Malone,
Lesley Raymer, Kieran Shekoni
Assistant Cast Coordinators, Volunteers
Genevieve Baker, Hannah Caple,
Joanna Griffith, Ellena Jones, Andrea
Mangerie, Diana Prociv, Solomon
Wilkinson Casting Assistants, Volunteers

Costume, Hair & Make-Up

Tahra Zafar Head of Costume,
Hair & Make-up
Catherine Hill
Costume Supervisor
Matthew George Hair & Wigs
Design Supervisor
Amber Sibley Make-up Design Supervisor
Katie Newitt Costume
Department Coordinator
Lesley-Ann Halls Costume Department
Volunteers Coordinator
Fiona Parker Assistant Costume Supervisor
Caroline Brett Senior Costume Buyer
Rebecca Mills, Samantha Langridge,
Charlotte McGarrie Costume Buyers
Vanessa Bastyan Costume Workshop Fabrication
Supervisor
Angie Pledge Costume Workshop Supervisor
Elaine Battye Costume Workshop
Senior Costumier
Becky Johnson, Thea Keenan
Costume Workshop Senior Fabricators
Cheryl Mason
Costume Breakdown Supervisor
Nicola Beales, Helena Bennett, Robin McGrorty
Costume Workshop Assistants
Maisie McCubbin Costume Workshop Junior
Olima Rolfe Creative Division Assistant
Jamie Mendonça
Garment Stock Logistics & Driver

Headline Talent

Mitch Kirsch, Charlie Venturi Headline Talent Managers
Rachel Downey, George Ibbetson Headline Talent Coordinators

Lighting & Audio Design

Patrick Woodroffe
Lighting Designer

Over the last 30 years,
Patrick has been
responsible for the lighting
of an extraordinary array of
people and places including
rock stars and opera
singers, ballet dancers and
ice skaters, kings, queens,
presidents and desert sheiks, military camps and palaces, forests
and waterfalls, racing cars, cruise liners and the World Cup.

*Patrick a assuré ces 30 dernières années l'éclairage d'un
extraordinaire éventail de personnalités et de lieux : stars du
rock et chanteurs d'opéra, danseurs de ballet et patineurs,
rois, reines, présidents et cheikhs du désert, camps militaires
et palais, forêts et cascades, voitures de course, paquebots
et Coupe du Monde.*

Bobby Aitken
Audio Designer

Bobby is a world-renowned
theatre sound designer. His
work includes worldwide
productions of *Ghost*,
Mamma Mia!, *Dirty Dancing*,
We Will Rock You and *Return
to the Forbidden Planet*.
Credits for large scale
in-the-round opera include *Carmen*, *Madame Butterfly*, *Aïda*,
Cavalleria Rusticana and *Pagliacci*, *Tosca* and *La Bohème*.

*Concepteur sonore de renommée mondiale pour le théâtre,
Bobby a collaboré aux productions mondiales de Ghost, Mamma
Mia!, Dirty Dancing, We Will Rock You et Return to the Forbidden
Planet. Il a également travaillé sur des opéras in-the-round de
grande envergure comme Carmen, Madame Butterfly, Aïda,
Cavalleria Rusticana, Pagliacci, Tosca et La Bohème.*

Adam Bassett
Associate Lighting
Designer
Scott Willsallen
Audio Systems
Designer

Discover more about the Ceremony, including exclusive videos at london2012.com/exploretheceremonies
Pour en savoir plus sur la cérémonie et découvrir des vidéos exclusives, rendez-vous sur london2012.com/exploretheceremonies

Production Team: Creative
Équipe de production créative

Mass Movement

Steve Boyd Head of Mass Movement Choreography & Parade of Athletes

Steve has contributed to 11 consecutive Summer and Winter Olympic Games from Barcelona 1992 to London 2012. Other credits include Special Olympics, Commonwealth Games, Cricket World Cup, Asian Games and Super Bowl halftime shows. Prior to event production, Steve designed for several Condé Nast publications including *Vanity Fair* and *The New Yorker*.

De Barcelone 1992 à Londres 2012, Steve a participé à 11 Jeux Olympiques d'été et d'hiver consécutifs. Il a également collaboré aux Jeux olympiques spéciaux, aux Jeux du Commonwealth, à la Coupe du monde de cricket, aux Jeux asiatiques et aux spectacles de la mi-temps du Super Bowl. Avant la production événementielle, Steve a exercé ses talents de designer pour plusieurs publications du groupe Condé Nast, dont Vanity Fair et The New Yorker.

Soha Frem, Gina Chan Martinez, Rocky Smith, Bryn Walters, Nikki Woollaston, Nathan Wright Mass Movement Leaders
Ben Clare, Laura-Anne Gill, Vicki Igbokwe, Jeanefer Jean-Charles, Natasha Khamjani, Katie Pearson, Barbarana Pons, Wendy Steatham Mass Movement Coordinators
Edwina Allen, Taylor Anthony, Rachelle Conroy, Marianne Howard, Sean Mulligan, Brenda Jane Newhouse, Darragh O'Leary, Joseph Pitcher, Simone Sault, Carla Trim-Vamben, Claira Vaughan, Jayde Westaby Mass Movement Assistants
Paul Neaum Manager, Parade of Athletes
Darrin Peters Assistant, Parade of Athletes

Design

Ala Lloyd Design Studio Manager
Emma Child Design Studio Coordinator
Basmah Arafeh, Rebecca Brower, Hatty Morris Design Studio Assistants

Producers
Sarah Currie Associate Producer

Over the last 20 years Sarah has produced a number of live events around the world including music, private and corporate events. She's been the Band Producer on the MTV Europe Music Awards for the last seven years.

Au cours des 20 dernières années, Sarah a dirigé de nombreux évènements de par le monde, événements musicaux, privés ou d'entreprise. Elle est productrice chargée des groupes pour les MTV Europe Music Awards depuis sept ans.

Annie Corrigan Production Coordinator & Protocol Manager
Hannah Davies Personal Assistant to Artistic Director

Music

Martin Koch Music Supervisor
Tom Jenkins Associate Music Supervisor
Clare Hazeldine Music Department Coordinator
Nick Gilpin Audio Supervisor
Toby Pitman, Rob Playford Music Programmers

Publications

Fiona Richards Publications Manager
Jess Anstee Publications Coordinator

Stage Management

Sam Hunter Production Stage Manager
Guido Foa Deputy Production Stage Manager
**Carola Altissimo, Liz Copp, Debbie Cronshaw,
Hilary Davis, Ben Delfont, Anthony Field,
Duane Harewood, Liz Holden, Marianne Kuehner,
Claire Loftus, Jordan Noble-Davies, Sam Pepper,
Helen Smith, Ian Stephenson, Jorge Tapia,
Peter Wakeman, Matt Watkins**
Senior Stage Managers
**Holly Anderson, Miriam Bertaina, Abigail Dankwa,
Miguel de la Fuente Graciani, Rhiannon Harper,
Gareth Hulance, Jones, Dominique Pierre-Louis,
Ryan Quelch, Kate Ramsey, Gemma Thomas**
Stage Managers
Abigail Mills Associate Stage Manager
Julia Whittle Show Caller

Video Content Design

Sam Pattinson Screen
Content Consultant Producer
Luke Halls Screen Content
Creative Director
Rhyannon Hanbury-Aggs
Screen Content Production
Manager
Jude Greenaway Director
See Me Feel Me shoot

Internship Placements Lexi Boynton, Andrew Clifford, Colm Dunhrosa,
Jacqueline Field, Amy Gibson, Elizabeth Howe, Lexi Hyland, Anisha Patel,
Janita Patel, Katie Radha Osterholzer, Claire Thorn, Daniel Vincze

Creative & Executive Administration

Tina Jaffray
Senior Administrator, Creative
Jennifer Hutt Executive Assistant to the
Head of Ceremonies and Executive Producer
Kate Hinchliffe Executive Assistant
to the Producers
Nicky Cheung Personal Assistant to
Director of Ceremonies,
Education & Live Sites
Veronique Haddelsey
Protocol Coordinator
Alison Wade Script Manager
Clare Ellis Administration Assistant
Lucy Moffat Runner

Production Team: Technical
Équipe de production technique

Technical Executive

Piers Shepperd
Technical Director

For 20 years, Piers has delivered technical production wizardry for mega events around the globe. Critically acclaimed projects in theatre and music include *We Will Rock You* and the Rolling Stones Licks World Tour. Other work includes the Athens 2004 Olympic Ceremonies, 2006 Doha Asian Games Ceremonies and 2010 Delhi Commonwealth Games Ceremonies.

Piers insuffle depuis 20 ans un peu de magie à la production technique des méga-événements de la planète. Encensés par la critique, les projets qu'il a réalisés dans les domaines du théâtre et de la musique comprennent We Will Rock You *et la tournée mondiale Licks des Rolling Stones. Il a également travaillé sur les cérémonies des Jeux Olympiques d'Athènes, en 2004, des Jeux asiatiques de Doha, en 2006, et des Jeux du Commonwealth de Delhi, en 2010.*

Andrew Morgan
Senior Administrator, Technical
Elena Dogani
Production Coordinator, Technical Contracts
Ross Nicholson
Production Assistant, Technical

Aerial & Special Projects

James Lee Technical Manager, Aerial & Special Projects
Glenn Bolton Senior Production Manager, Capital Works & Special Projects
Luke Mills Production Manager, Pyro, Flame & SFX
Edwin Samkin Deputy Production Manager, Pyro, Flame & SFX
Sammy Samkin Production Manager, Fireworks
Nick Porter Deputy Production Manager, Aerialist Training
Paul English Deputy Production Manager, Show Vehicles
Chris Vaughan Senior Production Manager, Staging, Scenic & Props
Zoe Buttling Deputy Production Manager
Emma Neilson Production Coordinator

Audio, Comms & Broadcast

Chris Ekers Senior Production Manager, Audio & Comms
James Breward Deputy Production Manager, Comms, CCTV & Mass Cast IEM
Alison Dale Deputy Production Manager, Principal Performer IEM & Wireless Mics
Trevor Beck Audio Playback
Gary Bradshaw Audio FOH
Steve Watson Audio Monitor Engineer
Steve Williams Audio Broadcast Systems Engineer
Andy Rose Audio Broadcast Sound Supervsior
Hannah Charlesworth
Deputy Production Manager, Backline

Lighting, AV & Power

Nick Jones Technical Manager, Lighting, AV & Power
Andy Loveday Senior Production Manager, Lighting
Ben Pitts Production Manager, Lighting Set LX
Dan Sloane Production Manager, Video & LED Screens
Tim Routledge Senior Lighting Operator
Andrew Voller Lighting Operator

Pryderi Baskerville Lighting Operator
Lee Threlfall Set Lighting Production LX
Dave Bartlett Project Manager, Pixels
Mike Dawes Deputy Project Manager, Pixels

Staging & Scenic

Jeremy Lloyd Technical Design & Staging Manager
Nigel Mousley Senior Production Manager, Staging & Scenic
Steve Richards Senior Production Manager, FOP
Chris Clay, Dave Williams Production Managers, Staging & Scenic
Kieran McGivern Deputy Production Manager, Staging & Scenic
Scott Seaton Deputy Production Manager, FOP
Mark Berryman Staging/Transition Manager
Rick Worsfold Head Set Carpenter
Phil Broad Senior Production Manager (Rigging)
Lianne Bruce Production Coordinator, Staging & Scenic

Johanna Eaden Production Assistant, Staging & Scenic
Tom White CAD Manager
Andrew Bailey, Ben O'Neill, Philip Wilding CAD Operators
Moose Curtis, Magnus Harding, Kevin Jones Staging Crew Chiefs
Peter English Head Carpenter
Phil Perry Staging Crew Chief, Rehearsal Venue
Ray Bogle Field of Play Crew Chief
Mike Grove Band Stage Manager
Rasti Bartek, Aran Chadwick, Glyn Trippick Consultant Engineers
Richard Bentley, John Prentice CAD Consultants

Technical Services

Scott Buchanan Technical Manager,
Technical Services & Special Projects
Annette Stock Production Manager, Schedule,
Crew & Contractors
Jess Noakes Production Coordinator, Technical Services
Dave Wilkie Production Manager, Plant & AP
Matthew Beardsley Production Coordinator, Crew & Logistics
Terry Hubble Production Staff Quartermaster
Laura Lloyd, Grant Peters Production Staff Runners

Workshop & Props

Ted Irwin Technical Manager, Workshop & Props
Dan Shipton Production Manager, Props
Pam Nichol Deputy Production Manager, Props & Rehearsals
Eric Hickmott Production Manager, Workshop
Rhiannon Newman-Brown Production Coordinator, Workshop
Nick Bloom Deputy Production Manager, Carpentry
Sherri Hazzard Deputy Workshop Manager, Props
Sally Christopher, Sean Flynn Production Coordinator, Props
Mark Moore Deputy Production Manager, Metal Fabrication

Internship Placements Laura Rixson, Chris Tani

Will Sumpter Deputy Workshop Manager, Props
Steve Dart, John McGarrigle Props, LX
John Pratt Workshop Coordinator & Buyer
Dave Blacker Props Coordinator and Crew &
Volunteer Chief
Stephen Jeffrey Crew & Volunteer Chief
Sarah Whiting Workshop Volunteer
Coordinator
Krissy Lee Technical Assistant

Production Team: Operations
Équipe de production opérationnelle

Operations Executive

Mik Auckland
Director of Operations and Health & Safety

A career as a stage manager and technical director in musical theatre led Mik to senior roles at the Sydney 2000 and Athens 2004 Olympic Games. In 2005 he joined Jack Morton Worldwide as Senior Technical Director. Mik subsequently worked on the Beijing 2008 Olympic Games and the 2010 FIFA World Cup as Consultant Technical and Operations Director.

Une carrière de régisseur et de directeur technique dans le théâtre musical a amené Mik à assumer des fonctions d'encadrement aux Jeux de 2000 à Sydney et de 2004 à Athènes. En 2005, il a rejoint Jack Morton Worldwide en tant que directeur technique senior. Mik a ensuite travaillé sur les Jeux Olympiques de 2008 à Pékin et sur la Coupe du monde de Football 2010 en tant que directeur technique et opérationnel consultant.

Adrian Bourke Senior Manager, Venues & Facilities
Joseph Frisina Senior Operations Manager
Donna McMahon Senior Manager, Logistics
Neil Russell Senior Manager, Health, Safety, Welfare & Medical
Hannah Dorey Senior Administrator
Nathan Farquharson Logistics Coordinator
Jacinta Gee Operations Coordinator
Luke Woodham Venues & Facilities Coordinator
Alice Larmer Logistics Production Assistant

Health, Safety, Welfare & Medical
Show Operations & Scheduling

Conrad Schwarz Deputy Manager, Health & Safety
Sally-Ann Dod Health & Safety Advisor, Inductions & Contractor Liaison
Sarah Jones Medical Services Manager
Danielle Bromley, Steve Brown, Alan Law Health & Safety Consultants
Samantha Coles Coordinator, Health & Safety
Sally Downey Health & Safety Inductions Assistant
Dean Jewel Show Operations & Schedule Manager
Paddy Bettington Show Operations & Schedule Assistant
Leah Harris, Sam Mount Schedule Production Assistants

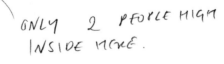

Logistics

Kirsty Thomson Operations Manager,
Catering, Cleaning & Waste
Julia Bowditch, Lynsey Jackson Coordinators, Catering,
Cleaning & Waste
**Rebecca Fletcher, Sandra Goetz, Gareth Lewis,
Ria Maycox, Alexander Thomas, Sarah Yates**
Production Assistants, Catering, Cleaning & Waste
Melissa McVeigh Operations Manager, Accreditation
Melanie East, Tyler Ffrench, Vincenzo Ianniello
Coordinators, Accreditation
Karen Cosgree, Emily Whitaker
Production Assistants, Accreditation
Laura Marakowits Operations Manager, Volunteers
Shelly Donaghy Coordinator, Volunteers
Grace Birkbeck, Laura Salvatore, Pete Thomson
Production Assistants, Volunteers
Valie Voutsa Operations Manager,
Accommodation & Travel
Leticia Gonzalez-Galvez Assistant Manager,
Accommodation & Travel (Principal Performers)
Eloise Crevier, Eirini Zoi
Production Assistants, Accommodation
Georgina Huxstep Operations Manager, Transport & Fleet
Sarah Hinchelwood Assistant Manager, Children's Transport
Matthew Howlett Assistant Manager, Fleet & Site Vehicles
Kate Blomfield, Asha Slade Coordinators, Transport
**Simon Galicki, Laura Gallen, Charlotte Howley,
Emma Lester, Emily Webber**
Production Assistants, Transport
Debbie Paul Operations Manager,
Principal Performer Logistics
Craig Lear Green Room Manager
Anna-Maria Kreuzer Coordinator, Principal Performer Logistics
Victoria Sandford, Kieran Smith, Ed Woodhouse
Production Assistants, Principal Performer Logistics

Venues & Facilities

Russel Bedford Operations Manager,
Workshop & Rehearsal Venues
Pete Williams Assistant Manager,
Rehearsal Venues
William Francis Coordinator, Workshop
& Rehearsal Venues
Sonya Gandras Coordinator, Rehearsal Venues
**Billy Cheeseman, Ralph Cullum,
Charlotte Jordan** Production Assistants, Venues
Robert Madeley, Isabel Uriach Site Assistants,
Rehearsal Venue
Lucinda Erskine-Crum Operations Manager,
Olympic Park
Al Parkinson Assistant Manager, Olympic Stadium
Toni Stockham Coordinator, Olympic Stadium
David Gregory Assistant Manager, Compound
Marcia Connell, Will Gunnett
Coordinators, Compound
Robert Schnaiberg Assistant Manager,
MDS, Storage & Freight

Sarah Adams, Olivia Pole-Evans
Site Assistants,
MDS, Storage & Freight
Lottie Cresswell
Assistant Manager, Common Domain
Chui-Yee Cheung
Coordinator, Common Domain
Ryan Tate Coordinator, Venue
Joanne Davis, Lily Sutton
Production Assistants, Venue
Eva Budd, Holly Gregory
Compound Assistants, Stadium
Trish Murphy
Venue Manager, Eton Manor
Claire Ewings
Assistant Venue
Manager, Eton Manor
**Kayleigh Dean,
Megan Wise** Venue
Assistants, Eton Manor

Internship Placements Tanisha Malkki, Dimitry Ragozin

Production Team: Administration
Équipe de production administrative

Administration Executive

Sara Donaldson
Joint Chief Operating Officer

Sara has overseen the delivery of many high-profile events and campaigns, including the bid for London 2012. In 2000 she set up LIVE Communications and was awarded an OBE. She co-founded Unspun in 2008 with whom she led the strategic direction of England's bid for the 2018 FIFA World Cup and co-produced the Glasgow 2014 Commonwealth Games Handover in Delhi.

Sara a supervisé la mise en œuvre de nombreux événements et campagnes prestigieux dont la candidature de Londres aux Jeux de 2012. En 2010, elle a créé LIVE Communications et a été faite Officier de l'empire britannique. En 2008, elle a été l'une des cofondatrices d'Unspun, avec qui elle a assuré la direction stratégique de la candidature de l'Angleterre à l'organisation de la Coupe du Monde de la FIFA 2018 et coproduit le passage à Glasgow 2014 des Jeux du Commonwealth à Delhi.

Chris Laue
Joint Chief Operating Officer

A key team member from the beginning of London 2012 Ceremonies, Chris has served as Procurement and Contracts Director, Board Director, Producer and Interim Chief Operating Officer. Prior to moving to London, he was Creative Producer/Director for LiveCity Vancouver, the city's live sites for the 2010 Olympic and Paralympic Winter Games.

Membre clé de l'équipe de London 2012 Ceremonies depuis le début, Chris a exercé les fonctions de directeur des achats et des contrats, de membre du conseil d'administration, de producteur et de directeur des opérations par intérim. Avant de s'intaller à Londres, il était producteur créatif et directeur pour LiveCity Vancouver, qui regroupe les sites accueillant les manifestations en direct des Jeux Olympiques et Paralympiques d'hiver de 2010.

Finance

Andrew Slater Financial Controller
Veronica Bailey Management Accountant
Kathleen Anderson Production Accountant
Mladen Ivezic, Farishta Yousuf
Senior Purchase Ledger Administrators
Hayden Porritt Purchase Ledger

Human Resources

Chidimma Chukwu Finance, Payroll & HR Clerk
Rebecca Janiszewska Human Resources Manager
Geraldine Daly, Derek Taylor, Cherise Scotland Human Resources Coordinators
Selina Donald Executive Assistant to Chief Operating Officer

Internship Placement **Christianne Gandossi**

Information Technology

Campbell McKilligan
Head of IT & Comms
Dilraj Sachdev Database Manager
Allan Whatmough Application Developer
Gyula Keresztely-Krall
System Administrator

Grant Cassin Mac Specialist
Saif Ahmed, Abdullah Al-Mamoon, Regis Joffre, Rica Mackay, Irfan Mohammed, Khizzar Younis Desktop Engineers
Marita Samuel IT Department Coordinator
Mick Turvey Service Desk Manager

Legal

Will Hutchinson Head of Legal (Culture, Ceremonies, Education & Live Sites)
Chris Loweth Senior Ceremonies Lawyer
Shirin Foroutan Senior Ceremonies Legal Advisor
Sarah Naisby Trainee Solicitor
Rachael Barrows Assistant Company Secretary

Procurement & Contracts

Simon Aspland
Head of Procurement & Contracts
Natalie Foster, Robert Graham, Ilyas Rahman, Stephanie Tillman, Marlon Trotman
Procurement & Contracts Administrators

Monique Pennycooke, Rachel Williams
Procurement & Contracts Coordinators
David Sugden Lawyer

Ceremonies, Education & Live Sites

Caroline Ainley Financial Control Accountant
Anna Blackman Programme Manager
Mark Smith Finance Manager
Kristina Richmond Procurement Manager

London 2012 Ceremonies Ltd

Scott Givens
Managing Director

Scott is an Olympic Ceremonies and mega-event producer with more than 300 spectaculars to his credit. Leading the team at creative production firm FiveCurrents, he has worked on 11 Olympic Games, and was awarded the prestigious Olympic Order. His productions have also received numerous Emmy Awards, Telly Awards and Sports Business Awards.

Scott est un producteur de cérémonies olympiques et de méga-événéments avec plus de 300 shows spectaculaires à son actif. Chef de file de la société de production créative FiveCurrents, il a travaillé sur 11 éditions des Jeux Olympiques et a reçu le prestigieux Ordre Olympique. Ses productions ont également remporté de nombreux Emmy Awards, Telly Awards et Sports Business Awards.

Board of Directors

Scott Givens (Chair)
Sara Donaldson
Martin Green
Chris Laue
Bill Morris
Catherine Ugwu
Frank McCormack (non-executive)
Alan Robertson (non-executive)

London 2012 Ceremonies Committee

Bill Morris (Chair)
Charles Allen
Doug Arnott
Jackie Brock-Doyle
Seb Coe
Paul Deighton
Martin Green
Will Hutchinson
Catherine Ugwu
Neil Wood

Production Credits
Générique de production

Special Thanks

AgustaWestland
BMW
British Fashion Council
Crystal CG
Dr. Martens
GoPro
Massey Ferguson
Samsung
Signature Systems Group
Site-Eye Time-Lapse Films
Swarovski
Trekinetic
Tumblr
VOGUE®

Acknowledgements

3 Mills Studios
English National Ballet
Prudence Cuming Ltd
Royal Ballet Upper School
Royal Opera House
Science Ltd
Omer Ali
Danielle Buckley
Sarah Casey
Lauren Cuthbertson
Keith Davey
Barry Gibb
Dwina Gibb
Melissa Hamilton
John Harkins
Kaz Hill
Simon Hilton
Damien Hirst
Yoko Ono
Amanda Softly
Patrick Stalder
Jude Tyrell

Artist Management

10 Management
Anglo Management
Asgard
Becker Brown
Brontone Management
Crown Talent
Decisive Management
Disturbing London
Empire Management
Hannah Management
IMG Artists
Jim Beach Management
John Noel Management
Lateral Management
Lippman Entertainment
Markham, Forggatt & Irwin
Modest Management
Outside Organisation
Quest Management
Rocket Music
Select Model Management
Storm Model Management
Supervision Management
TCB Group
Tess Management
Tony Smith Personal Management
TRC Management
Trinifold Management
XIX Entertainment

Assistant Stage Managers

Eleanor Butcher
Grace Cameron
Stuart Campbell
Shaun Corcoran
Henrietta Curtis
Anthony Earles
Chloe French
Gemma Friel
George Hims
Scarlett Hooper
Osnat Koblenz
Tom Leggat
Dan Miller
Connor Mitchell
Zanna Orage
Georgia Paget
Christopher Mark Smith
Phillipa Sutcliffe
Sarah Sweet
PK Thummukgool

Audience Pixel Content

Fillipo Bianchi
Will Case
Ed Cookson
Kate Dawkins
Giedre Domzaite
Neil Evan
Henry Flitton
Jude Greenaway
Jing Huang
Ray Lewis
Mark Lindner
Tom Lowndes
Giles Maunsell
Andrew McKinna
Pete Mellor
Chris Ratcliffe
Nicol Scott
Jamie Shiels
Martin Stacey
Zsuzsanna Voros
Catherine Woodhouse

Audio Visual

Hollywood Records
Paramount Pictures
Queen Productions Ltd
Treatment Studio
Universal Records
Sim Canetty-Clarke
Simon Hilton
Tom Moss
Max Tipple

British Fashion

Alexander McQueen
Burberry
Christopher Kane
Erdem
Jonathan Saunders
Paul Smith
Stephen Jones
Victoria Beckham
Vivienne Westwood

Broadcast

BBC
CTV Outside Broadcast
Done & Dusted
Olympic Broadcasting Services

Casting

Perform Health Physiotherapy
Royal Academy of Dance
Karen Calvert
Laci Endrez
Jian He
Steve Hough
Laura Jackson
Bally Kalsi
Jaz Kalsi
Steve McNicholas
Mike Roberts
Loretta Sacco
Craig Sherratt
Claire Slater
Julia Walter
Dan Whiston
Liang Yang

Costume

Acton Cut
Angels the Costumier
BFS Buttons
Cooper & Stollbrand Ltd
Empee Silks
FFGM
Freeds of London
Freidman's Ltd
Ivo Textile Ltd
Jane Anne Designs
Kwik Grade Ltd
Laceys
Nicola Killeen Textiles
Prestige Dyers
Print a Gift
Toumazi
Wear Moi
Western Supplies
Whaleys
Zone Creations
Robert Allsopp
Robert Hughes
Yasemin Kascigolu
Adam Keenan
Georgina Lamb
Daniel Marks
Cheryl Mason
Richard Pledge
Phil Reynolds
Reenell Roach-Williams
Marion Weise

Costume, Hair and Make-up Specialist Crew

Alex Babsky
Terry Barber
Jennifer Barnard
David Barton
Nikki Belding
Valerie Benavides
Veronica Buitrago-Martinez
Cathy Burczak
Sylvaine Champeau
Katy Cherry
Anna Cofone
Andrea Cracknell
Fay De Bremaeker
Sarah Deans
Ian Denson
Sarah Dickson
Hadeel El-Tal
Emma Fairfield
Liam Farrelly
Leon Fernholdt
Pam Foster
Oliver Gamblin
Val Garland

Mandy Gold
Karen Gurney
Cyndia Harvey
Gemma Hoff
Eamonn Hughes
Lauren Isles
Samantha Jones
Lizzie Judd
Marialena Kapotopoulou
Alexandra Kharibian
Shelley King
Sukie Kirk
Spencer Kitchens
Debbie Korrie
Charlotte Lander
Monica McDonald
Sam McKnight
Catherine McLoughlin
Kimberley Murray
Kirsteen Naismith
Emily Newbold
Marian Newman
Jo Nielsen
Tanya Noor
Jess O'Shea
Rose Octon
Marc Ramos
Jon Revell
Mary Richardson
Emiliano Sabariz
Amy Sachon
Margarida Santos
Emma Sheffield
Charlotte Simpson
Emma Slater
Elaine Solomon
Helen Spink
Mariella Spoto
Stephanie Staunton
Jane Stoner
David Stringer
Janine Summerhayes
Wendy Topping
Sékou Traore
Jo Tuplin
Gemma Vincent
Aurelie Vogt
Marian Wandrag
Laura Watkins
Isabelle Webley
Nicola Webley
Nicola Weir
Tracey Wells
Laura Wisinger
Jenna Wyatt

Design

4D modelshop
London Graphic Centre
Katerina Angelopolou
Misty Buckley
Cecilia Carey
Matt Deely
Lauren Ferrell
Bronia Housman
Jacqueline Pyle
Zoe Squire
Chiara Stephenson

Finance

Albert Goodman LLP
IT Associates Ltd

Human Resources

Beder-Harrison & Co

Information Technology

Adobe
Electranet
Jigsaw 24
Lesar
Netapp
Symantec

Legal & Clearances

Department for Education
Michael Simpkins LLP
Universal Music
Nion Hazell
Kate Penlington
Barbara Zamoyska

Music

Abbey Road Studios
Air Studios
Angel Studios
Hackney Colliery Band
The Household Division
Ceremonial State Band
London Symphony Orchestra
Urban Voices
Laurence Anslow
Jon Bailey
Tom Bailey
Chris Barrett
Rupert Coulson
Fiona Cruickshank
Olga Fitzroy
Ben Foster
Geoff Foster
Dave Hage
David William Hearn
Kathryn McDowell CBE
Adam Miller
John Prestage
Marc Stevens
Nick Wollage

Operations

British Waterways
Bunzl
Cabots
The Civil Aviation Authority
Corinthia Hotel
Ford Dagenham
Go Ahead
Gravis Capital Partners LLP (GSP)
Grosvenor Facilities Services Ltd
Hyatt Regency London - The Churchill
IDS Develop
JLAB
JLAR
London Borough of Barking and Dagenham Council
London Development Agency
NATS
Sam's Cars
Sanofi
Sheraton Park Tower
Tesco Bromley-by-Bow
West One

Procurement

Bravo Solutions

Task Force 27

Including representation from:
Government Olympic Executive
Greater London Authority
London 2012 Ceremonies Ltd
London Organising Committee of the Olympic & Paralympic Games Ltd
London Rail
London Underground
Metropolitan Police Service
Network Rail
Transport for London
Westminster City Council / London Councils

Technical
A Plant
Adler and Allan
Ainscough Crane Hire
Artem
Atelier One
Brilliant Stages
Bruce Banks Sails
Buro Happold
Cardiff Theatrical Services
Creative Technology
Delta Sound
Elstree Light & Power (ELP)
Factory Settings
FCT Flames
Fibreweb Geosynthetics
Fineline
Flying FX Ltd
Gallowglass
Global Design Solutions
Howard Eaton Lighting
H-Squared Electronics
Kimbolton Fireworks Ltd

Lee Warren
MTFX
Pfeifer
Power Logistics
PRG
PyroJunkies
Riedel Communications
Serious Stages
Service Graphics
Sheetfabs
Showforce
Showstars
Stage Co.
Stage One Creative Services Ltd
Steel Monkey Engineering
Tait Technologies
The Technical Department
Total Fabrications
Transam Trucking
Unique Creations
Unusual Rigging Ltd
WiCreations

Technical Specialist Crew
Guy Aldridge
Chris Aram
Colin Armitage
Gibson Arpino
Sam Augustus
Hamish Bamford
Mark Berryman
Natasha Bingham
Aico Boshoven
Francesca Boyle
Chris Bray
Nick Breen
Phil Broad
Zoe Buttling
Darren Davidson
Dan Evans
Stuart Farnell
Luis Fernando Garcia
Pete Geary
Jason Gilbert
Alex Hatton
Martin Hinkins

Mike Howson
Linford Hudson
Kevin Jones
Steve Joy
Jem Matthews
Cattrina Mott
Rebecca Nelson
Jem Nicholson
Chris Patton
Colin Raby
Simon Rackham
Michael Scott
Nick Spalding
Barrie Spittles
Stephen Spittles
Pauline Stone
Scott Turnbull
Zoe Walker
Rachel Walsh
Richard Wearing
Oliver Welsh
Robert Woodley
Rick Worsfold

Music Credits
Générique musique

Dances with Wolves
Performed by London
Symphony Orchestra
Orchestra conducted by
Steve Sidwell
Written by Barry
EMI Music Publishing Ltd

Read All About It
Performed by Emile Sandé,
Gavin Powell
Emile Sandé appearing
courtesy of Virgin Records
Limited
Written by James/Barnes/
Kelleher/Kohn
SonyATV Music Publishing/
Bucks Music Group Ltd/
EMI Music Publishing Ltd

Because
Performed by Stomp, Urban
Voices
Written by Lennon/
McCartney
SonyATV Music Publishing

Salut d'Amour
Performed by Julian Lloyd
Webber, London Symphony
Orchestra
Orchestra conducted by
Steve Sidwell
Arranged by David Cullen
Written by Elgar

Fanfare
Performed by The Household
Division Ceremonial State
Band
Written by Jacobs

**God Save the Queen
(National Anthem)**
Performed by London
Symphony Orchestra,
Urban Voices
Orchestra conducted by
Steve Sidwell

'There's always something happening and it's usually quite loud'

Our House
Performed by Madness,
Joseph Auckland, Stephanie
Benedetti, Stephen Hamilton,
Natalie Holt, Michael
Kearsey, Rachael Lander,
Kirsty Mangan, London
Symphony Orchestra string
section
Orchestra conducted by
Steve Sidwell
Written by Foreman/Smythe
EMI Music Publishing Ltd

Park Life
Performed by The
Household Division
Ceremonial State Band
Written by Albarn/Coxon/
James/Rowntree
EMI Music Publishing Ltd

'East End boys and West End girls'

West End Girls
Performed by Pet Shop Boys,
appearing courtesy of
Parlophone Records
Written by Tennant/Lowe
SonyATV Music Publishing

What Makes You Beautiful
Performed by One Direction,
appearing courtesy of Syco
Music/Sony Music
Written by Kotecha/Yacoub/
Faulk
EMI Music Publishing Ltd/
Kobalt Music Publishing/
BMGChrysalis Music
Publishing

A Day in the Life
London Symphony
Orchestra
Orchestra conducted by
Steve Sidwell
Written by Lennon/
McCartney

'As long as I gaze on Waterloo sunset, I am in paradise'

Waterloo Sunset
Performed by Ray Davies,
London Symphony
Orchestra, Urban Voices
Orchestra conducted by
Steve Sidwell
Written by Davies
Publishing Carlin Music Corp

Read All About It (reprise)

Parade of Athletes
Performed by London
Symphony Orchestra
Conducted by Steve Sidwell
Written by Arnold

Open Arms
Performed by Elbow, London
Symphony Orchestra, Urban
Voices
Orchestra conducted by
Steve Sidwell
Written by Garvey/Jupp/
Potter/Potter

'One day like this'

One Day Like This
Performed by Elbow, London
Symphony Orchestra, Urban
Voices
Orchestra conducted by
Steve Sidwell
Written by Garvey/Jupp/
Potter/Potter

**Running Up That Hill
(A Deal with God Remix)**
Kate Bush
Drums: The Dhol Foundation
Written by Bush

'Sun, sun, sun, here it comes'

Here Comes the Sun
Performed by The Dhol Foundation, Urban Voices, Bilwa Iyer, Pete Lockett, Radha Meta, Chandrima Misra, Prabhat Rao, Guru Smt, Varun Verma
Written by Harrison

'Is this the real life?'

Bohemian Rhapsody
Queen
Written by Mercury
EMI Music Publishing Ltd
Courtesy of Universal-Island Records Ltd
Under License from Universal Music Operations Ltd

'I'm a dreamer, but I'm not the only one'
'Imagine all the people'

Imagine
John Lennon
Performed by Liverpool Philharmonic Youth Choir, Liverpool Signing Choir, London Symphony Orchestra
Orchestra conducted by Steve Sidwell
Written by Lennon
© Lenono Music

Freedom 90
Performed by George Michael, London Symphony Orchestra
George Michael appearing courtesy of Universal-Island Records a division of Universal Music Operations Limited
Written by Michael

White Light
Performed by George Michael, London Symphony Orchestra, Urban Voices
George Michael appearing courtesy of Universal-Island Records a division of Universal Music Operations Limited
Written by Michael

'From Soho down to Brighton'

Pinball Wizard
Performed by the Kaiser Chiefs
Written by Townshend
Published by Fabulous Music Ltd

Space Oddity
David Bowie
Written by Bowie
Licensed courtesy of RZO Music
Published by Tintoretto Music/RZO Music Ltd / Bucks Music Group Ltd

Changes
David Bowie
Written by Bowie
Licensed courtesy of RZO Music
Published by Tintoretto Music/RZO Music Ltd / EMI Music Publishing Ltd / Fairwood Music (UK) Ltd/ BMG Chrysalis Music Ltd

Ziggy Stardust
David Bowie
Written by Bowie
Licensed courtesy of RZO Music
Published by Tintoretto Music/RZO Music Ltd / EMI Music Publishing Ltd / Fairwood Music (UK) Ltd/ BMG Chrysalis Music Ltd

The Jean Genie
David Bowie
Written by Bowie
Licensed courtesy of RZO Music
Published by Tintoretto Music/RZO Music Ltd / EMI Music Publishing Ltd / Fairwood Music (UK) Ltd/ BMG Chrysalis Music Ltd

Rebel Rebel
David Bowie
Written by Bowie
Licensed courtesy of RZO Music
Published by Tintoretto Music/RZO Music Ltd / EMI Music Publishing Ltd / Fairwood Music (UK) Ltd/ BMG Chrysalis Music Ltd

Diamond Dogs
David Bowie
Written by Bowie
Licensed courtesy of RZO Music
Published by Tintoretto Music/RZO Music Ltd / EMI Music Publishing Ltd / Fairwood Music (UK) Ltd/ BMG Chrysalis Music Ltd

Young Americans
David Bowie
Written by Bowie
Licensed courtesy of RZO Music
Published by Tintoretto Music/RZO Music Ltd / EMI Music Publishing Ltd / Fairwood Music (UK) Ltd/ BMG Chrysalis Music Ltd

Let's Dance
David Bowie
Written by Bowie
Licensed courtesy of RZO Music
Published by Tintoretto Music/RZO Music Ltd / Fairwood Music (UK) Ltd

Music Credits
Générique musique

'We are the goon squad and we're coming to town, beep-beep'

Fashion
David Bowie
Written by Bowie
Licensed courtesy of RZO Music
Published by Tintoretto Music/RZO Music Ltd / EMI Music Publishing Ltd / Fairwood Music (UK) Ltd

'I wish that I could be that bird and fly away from here'

Little Bird
Performed by Annie Lennox
Steve Barney, Tony Remy, Bernie Smith, Mike Stevens, Paul Turner, The Company Drummers
Written by Lennox/Stewart
Universal Music Publishing Ltd

'Two lost souls swimming in a fish bowl'

Wish You Were Here
Performed by Richard Jones, Nick Mason, Mike Rutherford, Ed Sheeran
Written by Waters

Pure Imagination
Performed by Russell Brand, London Symphony Orchestra
Written by Newley/Bricusse

I am the Walrus
Performed by Bond, Russell Brand
Written by Lennon/McCartney
SonyATV Music Publishing

Right Here Right Now
Performed by Fatboy Slim
Written by Cook/Terry/Barry
Licensed courtesy of Skint Records
Universal Music Publishing Ltd

'Check it out now, the funk soul brother'

Rockerfella Skank
Performed by Fatboy Slim
Written by Cook/Peters/Walsh
Licensed courtesy of Skint Records
Universal Music Publishing Ltd/EMI Music Publishing Ltd

Price Tag
Performed by Jessie J, appearing courtesy of Lava / Universal Republic Records
Written by Gottwald/Cornish/Kelly/Simmons

Written in the Stars
Performed by Tinie Tempah, appearing courtesy of Parlophone Records
Written by Bernardo/Mughal/Okogwu/Turner

Dynamite
Performed by Taio Cruz, appearing courtesy of Universal-Island Records a division of Universal Music Operations Limited
Written by Cruz/Grottwald/Levin/Martin/McKee
EMI Music Publishing Ltd / Kobalt Music Publishing

'You should be dancing, yeah'

You Should Be Dancing
Performed by Taio Cruz, Jessie J, Tinie Tempah
Taio Cruz appearing courtesy of Universal-Island Records a division of Universal Music Operations Limited. Jessie J appearing courtesy of Lava / Universal Republic Records. Tinie Tempah appearing courtesy of Parlophone Records
Written by Gibb/Gibb/Gibb
Licensed courtesy of Warner Music UK Ltd

'All the colours of the world'

Spice Up Your Life
Performed by The Spice Girls
Written by Stannard/Rowe/Brown/Beckham/Bunton/Halliwell/Chisholm
EMI Music Publishing Ltd/Universal Music Publishing Ltd

Wannabe
Performed by The Spice Girls
Written by Stannard/Rowe/Brown/ Beckham/Bunton/Halliwell/Chisholm
EMI Music Publishing (WP) Ltd/Universal Music Publishing Ltd

Wonderwall
Performed by Beady Eye
Written by Gallagher
SonyATV Music Publishing

Mr Blue Sky
Electric Light Orchestra
Written by Lynne
EMI Music Publishing Ltd

'For life is quite absurd'

Always Look on the Bright Side of Life
Performed by Eric Idle, Susan Bullock, Blackheath Morris, Hackney Colliery Band, London Welsh Rugby Club Choir, London Welsh Male Voice Choir, Reading Scottish Pipe Band
Written by Idle

'I'll light the fuse and I'll never lose'

Survival
Performed by Muse, appearing courtesy of Warner Music
Written by Bellamy

Brighton Rock
Performed by Queen
Written by May
EMI Music Publishing Ltd

'Waving your banner all over the place'

We Will Rock You
Performed by Queen, Jessie J
Jessie J appearing courtesy of Lava / Universal Republic Records
Written by May
EMI Music Publishing Ltd

National Anthem of Greece
London Philharmonic Orchestra
Arranged by Philip Shepard
Universal Music

Olympic Anthem
Performed by London Welsh Male Voice Choir and London Welsh Rugby Club Choir
English lyrics by W Earl Brown and Shirley Russ
French lyrics by Jim Corcoran
Written by Samaras/Palamas

National Anthem of Brazil
London Philharmonic Orchestra
Arranged by Philip Shepard
Universal Music

Spirit of the Flame
Performed by London Symphony Orchestra, Metro Voices
Orchestra conducted by Steve Sidwell
Written by Arnold

'They're lighting up the sky tonight'

Rule the World
Performed by Take That, London Symphony Orchestra, Marcus Byrne, Donovan Hepburn, Milton McDonald, Lee Pomeroy, Bernie Smith, Mike Stevens
Take That appearing courtesy of Polydor Orchestra conducted by Steve Sidwell
Written by Donald/Orange/Barlow/Owen
EMI Music Publishing Ltd./SonyATV Music Publishing/Universal Music Pubishing Ltd

Baba O'Riley
Performed by The Who
Morgan Nicholls, William Nicholls, Chris Stainton, Zak Starkey, Simon Townshend
Written by Townshend
Published by Fabulous Music Ltd

See Me, Feel Me
Performed by The Who
Morgan Nicholls, William Nicholls, Chris Stainton, Zak Starkey, Simon Townshend
Written by Townshend
Published by Fabulous Music Ltd

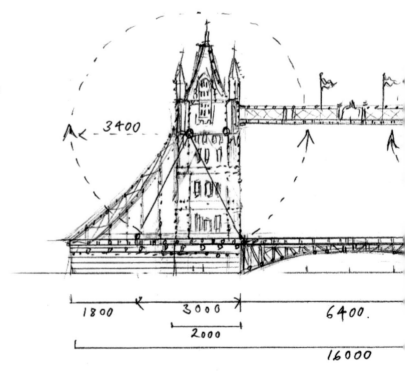

'Listening to you, I get the music'

Listening to You
Performed by The Who, Morgan Nicholls, William Nicholls, Chris Stainton, Zak Starkey, Simon Townshend
Written by Townshend
Published by Fabulous Music Ltd

'I'm not trying to cause a big s-s-sensation'

'I'm just talkin' 'bout my g-g-generation'

My Generation
Performed by The Who, Morgan Nicholls, William Nicholls, Chris Stainton, Zak Starkey, Simon Townshend
Published by Fabulous Music Ltd

There are snippets of songs throughout the Ceremony. The complete list will be credited online at london2012.com/exploretheceremonies

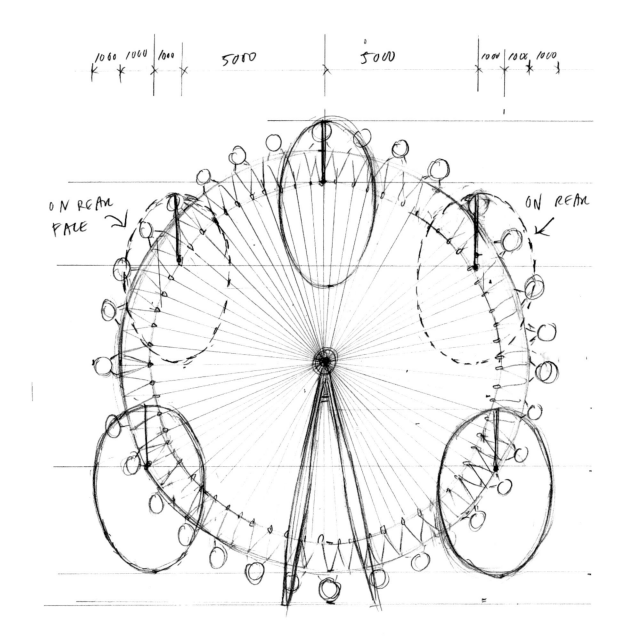

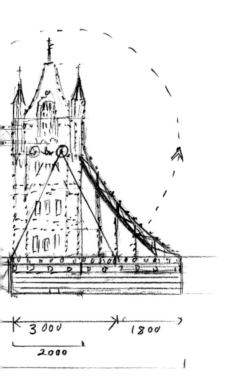

Clearance Credits
Autorisations

Film & Television

The characters, script and direction from the television series *Only Fools and Horses* (episode 'Heroes and Villains' TX 25/12/96) used with kind permission of the BBC, Shazam Productions and the family of the late John Sullivan.
The Trotters van from the television series *Only Fools and Horses* used with kind permission of the BBC.
The Italian Job courtesy of Paramount Pictures.

General

30 St Mary Axe (widely known as 'The Gherkin') used with permission of the owners of the building.
Battersea Power Station used with permission of the owners of Battersea Power Station.
EDF Energy London Eye conceived and designed by Mark Barfield Architects used with permission by the London Eye Company Ltd.
London Underground train IPR used by kind permission of Transport for London.
Batman and Robin costumes ™ & © DC Comics, used with the permission of Warner Bros Consumer Products, a division of Warner Bros Entertainment UK Ltd.

Literary works

Extract from *Mad Dogs and Englishmen* © NC Aventales AG 1931 by permission of Alan Brodie Representation Ltd.
Extract from *A Clockwork Orange* © the Estate of Anthony Burgess 2012.
Extract from *Charlie and the Chocolate Factory* by Roald Dahl is reproduced with the permission of Roald Dahl Nominee Ltd.
'Prayer' is taken from *Mean Time* by Carol Ann Duffy published by Anvil Press Poetry in 1993.
Extracts from 'The Waste Land' and 'The Hollow Men' taken from *Collected Poems 1909-1962* © Estate of TS Eliot and reprinted by permission of Faber and Faber Ltd.
Extract from 'Howards End' by EM Forster (© The Estate of EM Forster) is reproduced by permission of Peters Fraser & Dunlop on behalf of the Estate of EM Forster.
Extract from *The Go-Between* by LP Hartley reproduced with permission of The Society of Authors as the literary representative of the Estate of LP Hartley and with permission of Penguin Books.
Text by AA Milne © The Trustees of the Pooh Properties reproduced with permission of Curtis Brown Limited, London and The Walt Disney Company.
Extract from 'The Lion and the Unicorn' by George Orwell, reprinted with permission by AM Heath and Company.
Extract from *Look Back in Anger* by John Osborne reproduced with permission from the Arvon Foundation.
'A Martian Sends a Postcard Home' by Craig Raine, © Craig Raine, 1979, reproduced with permission of David Godwin Associates.
Extract from *Love in a Cold Climate* by Nancy Mitford © Nancy Mitford, reproduced by permission of the Estate of Nancy Mitford c/o Rogers, Coleridge & White Ltd.
Extract from *Pygmalion* by George Bernard Shaw reproduced with permission of The Society of Authors on behalf of the Bernard Shaw Estate.
Extract from 'Do Not Go Gentle into that Good Night' by Dylan Thomas, from *The Poems of Dylan Thomas*, © 1952 by Dylan Thomas, reprinted by permission of New Directions Publishing Corp and The Trustees for the Copyrights of Dylan Thomas, c/o David Higham Associates.
Quotation from JRR Tolkien's *The Lord of the Rings* © Fourth Age Limited 1954, 1966.
Extract from *Doctor Sally* by PG Wodehouse © PG Wodehouse, reproduced by permission of the Estate of PG Wodehouse c/o Rogers, Coleridge & White Ltd.

Photographs & Footage

Photographs of David Bowie – Courtesy of Terry O'Neill © Terry O'Neill
Courtesy of Mick Rock © Mick Rock, 1972, 2012
By Sukita courtesy of RZO Music / Sukita / The David Bowie Archive™
By Steve Schapiro courtesy of RZO Music / The David Bowie Archive™
By Carolyn Djanogly courtesy of RZO Music / The David Bowie Archive™.
Getty Images.
British Fashion photographs © Nick Knight.
Footage from 'Imagine' performed by John Lennon licensed courtesy of Yoko Ono Lennon.
Photograph of John Lennon by Iain Macmillan © Yoko Ono Lennon.

Images licensed under shutterstock.com.

Programme

Action Images.
Alamy.
Ian Britton.
'Who's Who' section photographs of Lily Cole, Lily Donaldson, Jourdan Dunn, Kate Moss © British *Vogue* / Condé Nast Publications Ltd.
Corbis.
Laspata DeCaro.
Sarah Dyson.
Max Ellis.
Christaan Felber.
Getty Images.
Cover design by Heatherwick Studio.
International Olympic Committee.
British Fashion photographs © Nick Knight.
Robert M Knight.
Sarah Langley.
Photograph of John Lennon by Iain Macmillan © Yoko Ono Lennon.
LOCOG.
Naomi Lowe.
Dan Martensen.
Steven Meisel.
Debra Musman.
Mike Owen.
NASA.
Press Association Images.
Jenny Quiggin.
Rex Features.
Trevor Roberts/BPM Media.
Grant Sainsbury.
Shutterstock.

If you'd like this programme in another language or format please email info@enquiries.london2012.com or phone +44 (0)845 267 2012 quoting LOC2012/CER/1382.

Published under license from London 2012 by Haymarket Network, Teddington Studios, Broom Road, Teddington, Middlesex TW11 9BE. Tel +44 (0)20 8267 5000. Reprinting in whole or in part is forbidden except with prior permission of the publisher. Due care is taken to ensure that the content of this programme is accurate, but the publisher and printer cannot accept liability for errors, omissions or alterations. Additionally, Ceremonies Producers acknowledge the contribution of anyone involved in the Ceremony whose name does not appear in the programme due to publication deadlines. Any alterations or additions to the credits will be available online at london2012.com/exploretheceremonies.

Printed at an environmentally aware ISO14001 printer on FSC® certified paper.

Si vous souhaitez obtenir ce programme dans une autre langue ou sous un autre format, veuillez envoyer un e-mail à l'adresse info@enquiries. london2012.com ou appelez le +44 (0)845 267 2012 en indiquant LOC2012/CER/1382.

Publié sous licence de Londres 2012 par Haymarket Network, Teddington Studios, Broom Road, Teddington, Middlesex TW11 9BE. Tél. +44 (0)20 8267 5000. Reproduction totale ou partielle interdite sans autorisation préalable de l'éditeur. Malgré les efforts pour garantir l'exactitude du contenu de ce programme, l'éditeur et l'imprimeur ne peuvent être tenus responsables des erreurs, omissions ou altérations qui pourraient y figurer. Les producteurs reconnaissent en outre la contribution de tout participant à la cérémonie dont le nom n'apparaîtrait pas dans le présent programme en raison des délais de publication. Toutes les modifications ou les ajouts aux crédits seront consultables en ligne sur london2012.com/exploretheceremonies.

Imprimé sur papier certifié FSC chez un imprimeur certifié ISO14001 sensibilisé aux questions environnementales.

FSC
www.fsc.org
MIX
Paper from responsible sources
FSC® C013417

Volunteers
Bénévoles

Pre-Show Lucy Abrahams, Angela Adler, Doreen Agyei, Marian Agyeman, Vivienne Ahmad, Minhaj Ahmed, David Alli-Balogun, Praveen Amarasinghe, Komal Amin, Clare Anderson, Faye Andrews, Vicky Annand, Niellah Arboine-Todd, Dioni Arvanitaki, Lorna Asante, Paul Ashby, Sophie Ashdown, Nicolas Ashwood, Tania Austin Herdman, Sola Awoberu, Tessa Baartmans, Amanda Bailey, Julia Bailey, Lucy Baker, Tatiana Baratto, Sonja Barber, Cassandra Bardot, Ursula Barzey, Michael Beard, Kate Beeching, Gabi Beer, Geoff Bell, Kate Bennett, Gloria Bernard, Anne-Marie Bevan, Sana Bhadelia, Varun Bhanot, Lynn Blackman, Oliver Blackman, Kat Blake-Pink, Katherine Blightman, Wendy Blow, Elisa Bodden, Lydia Bolwell, Emma Bond, Laura Bonifacii, Rhiannon Brace, Penny Breia, Hannah Broad, Elizabeth Brooks, Larissa Brown, Camilla Brueton, Julie Bryant, Kirsty Bullen, Katy Burke, Richard Burke, Mulgrew Cameron, Annie Campbell, June Campbell, Amy Carrick, Nicola Carsons, Finn Casey, Danielle Chamberlain, Chor Hon Chan, Ann Charles, Qi Chen, Nazish Choudhury, Luke Christie, Lauren Coates Lewis, Bianca Cole, Annie Coleman, Anne Corbett, Penny Costa, Anne Costello, Sarah Cowan, Lois Crane, Claire Cranmer, Cristiane Crauford, Gillian Dacey, Eleni Danika, Leaphia Darko, Carol Davis, Miranda Dawkins, Rhiannon Daye, Cara de Reuck, Barbara De Rios, Magnus Dearness, Maryam Delavar, Zu Ning Ding, Amada Dorta Cerpa, Jane Dotzek, Rachel Drew, Thorsten Dreyer, Adrian Dutch, Kara Earl, Insiah Edgecombe, Georgia Emm, Marialaura Ena, Jason Eustice, Christina Farley, Victoria Farmer, Madeleine Field, Liz Findlay, Ann Foley, Cabe Franklin, Arnold Frazer, Feonia French, Emma Fuller, Sonja Garsvo, Fiona Gaze-Fitzgibbon, Annie Gleeson, Graciete Gomes De Pina Costa, Serena Gonsalves-Fersch, Claudia Gonzalez Burguete, Juliet Goulding, Rhian Greaves, Aprille Green, Steve Griffin, Jan Halloran, Lynsey Hamilton, Beatrice Harbour, Penelope Harris, Carole Hayward, Felicity Hearn, Naomi Heathcote, Rosemary Henderson, Emily Herrett, Amy Hession, Grace Hewitt, Jan Hickman, Anna Hirst, Clare Hodgkin, Cynthia Holness, Veronica Hooles, Ellen Hooper-Doku, Jonathan Hoxby, Michelle Hsieh, Kellie Hughes, Nicola Hunter, Susan Innes, Judith Irwin, Wioletta Jablonska, Ian Jacobsberg, Sue James, Amy Jankiewicz, Yvette Jarvis, Judy Jenkin, Xiya Jia, Jo Johnson, Cat Jones, Jill Jordan, Lydia Julien, Teresa Kennedy, Aida Khalil Gomez, Montserrat Kidwell, Suzanne King, Alex Kolton, Ursula Kopp, Silvia La Greca Bertacchi, Laura Lagana, Jenny Laidlaw, Kirsten Laird, Heidi Latronico-Ferris, Elaine Lau, Ana Lavekau, Hilary Lawrence, Van Le, Julia Lee, Camilla Leonelli, Sok Leong, Michael Lesirge, Dez Lewis, Sisi Li, Manila Lippi, Jingjing Liu, Nicola Lloyd, Tracy Lodge, Fabia Lonnquist, Mia Lowry, Julie Lung, Katherine Lynch, Rachel Lyons, Sacha Mandel, King Mason, Michael Mcauliffe, Angela Mcintosh, Marie Mclernon, Kate Mcswiney O'Rourke, Hema Mehta, Dom Melaragni, Charlene Michael, Lina Michael-Imobioh, Jeffrey Miller, Madeleine Mills, Sally Mills, Pam Milsom, Chris Minton, Margaret Mitchell, Hannah Mizon, Jasvir Singh Modaher, Natalie Mooney, Mary Morrell, Natasha Morrison-Osbourne, Anusha Muhundan, Lesley Mulley, Nicky Mutale, Muhammed Neeliyath, Demelza Nelson, Stan Onyejekwe, Julie Oram, Karen Orwell, Natalie Osei-Owusu, Sabrina Oufella, Amy Page, Jyoti Patel, Sharron Patrick, Debra Payne, Jennifer Payne, Sarah Payne, Laura Pethers, Andrea Phillips, Therese Pickard Price, Rebecca Pinder, Michel Pinte, Pearl Prashar, Rachel Pratt, Stephen Pretty, Hannah Pyper, Hema Raghwani, Heenal Raichura, Shanmugapriya Raju, Suzanne Read, Shayne Reason, Fiona Reid, Thomas Richards, Cheryl Richardson, Angela Riches, Maria Rosiak, June Rowlands, Vicky Royall, Mayra Ruiz, Davina Russell, Shereen Russell, Lois Russell-Moyle, Zahida Saddiq, Christina Sage, Victoria Salcevich, Nathalie Salic, Jasvin Sanghera, Buledy Sangwa, Denise Savill, Natalie Schofield, Lorayne Seaholme, Rutu Shah, Sonia Shah, Caterina Shepherd, Fiorenza Shepherd, Ingrid Shiel, Alex Sierra Rodriguez, Maria Sierra-Negrete, Joao Roberto Silva Barros, Mandy Simpson, Nisha Sivalingam, Anna Slater, Lauren Smithers, Luella Solomon, Mim Spettigue, Philly Spurr, Leili Sreberny-Mohammadi, Tracy Stedman, Elizabeth Stevenson, Azul Strong, Janet Ann Sullivan, Penelope Summers, Lucy Sutton, Jonathan Sweeney, Carole Swift, Paul Tame, Hellen Thatcher, Anjila Thomas, Carmenleta Thomas, Helen Thomas, Donna Africa Thompson, Amanda Thorne, Angela Tomkinson, Victoria Tucker, Silviya Valkova, Jose Antonio Vazquez Mata, Natalia Velaz Ripa, Caroline Viple, Charlotte Vowden, Andy Wakeford, Samantha Walker, Sarah Walker, Rebecca Wallace, Rachel Wedderburn, Polly Wells, Bernadine Williams, Lorraine Williams, Clare Wills, Kirsty Witherden, Chris Wolff, Gulfem Wormald, Nelia Yakupova, Jun Yang, Carlotta Yannopoulou, Sarah Yarrall, Rosalind Zeffertt, Cen Zhang, Min Zhou, Julie Zhu **Rush Hour** Elspeth Adam, Madeleine Adams, Joseph Adelakun, Niji Adeleye, Derek Aidoo, Shakarah Alexis-Wilson, Charlotte Allchorne, Emily Allen, Harriet Allen, Laura Allsobrook, Ami Amlani, Nichole Anderson, Alicia Andrew, Constantinos Andronikou, Roberto Angrisani, Harriet Anscombe, Paul Archer, Natalia Magdalena Artemiuk, Rachel Ashby, Katie Bamforth, Naomi Barber, Lucy Barlow, Trudianne Bedward, Stephen Fabman-Beker, Adrian Benn, Cami Bennett, Rachel Bernard, Rhiannon Bevan, Rochelle Bisson, Kara Black, Jana Blagojevic, Jenni Blow, Christopher Boobyer, Chris Brind, Karl Brown, Mark Brown, Adriana Brown, Gilly Bruce, Irish Bumanglag, John Bunner, Emma Burford, Dan Burgess, Emma Butler, Andrew Bye, Stedroy Cabey, Emma Cahill, Zoe Caldwell, John Cannon, Linda Carlton, Sarah Chakaveh, Kathryn Chapman, Nicola Chatfield, Doug Cheshire, Yvonne Chisese, Amrit Chott, Mariesa Clarke, Holly Clarke, Oscarine Claude, Rebecca Comerford, Zoe Corbishley, Ellen Coulton, Yasmine Cumberbatch, Emma Cuthbert, Marianna Danilova, Michele Carmine Dato, Debbie Day, Gianluca De Martini, Shauniel Dean, Kirk Deighton, Petula Dennis, Gurinder Dhillon, Valerio Di Rocco, Helen Ding, John Dixon, Laura Douglas, Veronica Duffy, Claire Durrant, Beth Edmundson, Rebecca Edwards, Alex Eley, Maxine Eley, Lyrissa English, Cindy Evans, Rowena Evans, Grethe Febres-Cordero, Joanne Ferguson, Karin Floengaard Joensson, Joanna Forest-Jones, Ben Fox, Rebecca Francis, Andy Garrett, Fatima Gholizadeh, Naomi Gibb, Amina Gichinga, Michaela Gogova, Rachel Goode, Victoria Goodings, Kat Grabher, Shanice Grant-Barnett, Tonia Green, Laurence Greenhalgh, Sophie Grogan, Alice Haigh, Yasmin Halil, Xanthe Harding, Hilary Harvey, Rachael Hendrickson, Anthea Henry, Mae Hewitt, Louise Higgins, David Hill, Cliff Hilton, Sarah Hinds, Tim Hixson, Chelcee Hodgetts, Penelope Holmes, Ste Hopps, Nicholas Howe, Bob Hubbard, Daniel Huckle, Naomi Huggins, Charlotte Humphreys, Clarence Hunte, Ruth Ifode, Alice Jackson, Matthew Francis James, Julia Janikova, Benjamin Jervis, Coreen John, Sureya John, Andrew Johnson, Janine Johnson, Shaun Johnson, Jamila Jones, Patrice Kamurasi, Simone Kaye, Becks Kaysen, Louise Keen, Lucy King, Mary King, Jerry Knight, Matt Knight, Sarah Kosar, Kat Kowalczyk, Jennifer Krol, Fiona Kussy, Dacio Lamounier, Cara Latty, Rachel Lawrence, Rachel Layton, Hermione Leach, Chrystal Lecointe, Robert Legerwood, Hollie Leitch, Natasha Limbu, Rachel Lloyd, Kim Longbon, Hannah Longworth, Philly Lopez, Faye Lord, John Lynch, Marian Lynch, Sarah Mackey, Adrian Malthouse, Christian Marcazzo, Alison Marrs, Emma Martinelli, Alex Maslen, Steven Mason, Rachel Matthews, Patrick Mccann, Annie Mcconville, Alex Mccormick, Becky Mccormick, Samirah Mcdonald-Anderson, Marie Mcgonigle, John Mclaughlin, Heather Mclellan, Clare Meeking, Laura Mercer, Shelley Meredith, Mahatma Michael, Naomi Miller, Juan Jose Mohamed Bourgeois, Christina Molloy, Greg Monga, Alex Montaque, Jon Morales, Nathaniel Morrison, Stephen Mowbray, Jessica Mules, Chirag Mulia, Melanie Mullin, Scarlett Mullis, Cassie Murphy, Rutendo Mushambi, Ram Mylvaganam, Vicki Nash, Chip Nazmi, Tim Neale, Philippa Newis, Kelly Nicholas, Laura Ninou Teruel, Frank Noble, Vivian Nwonka, John Olding, Roberto Oliveira, Lizzie Orekoya, Ishia Osborne, Celia Osuagwu, Rhiain O'Sullivan, Alan Page, Cameron Palmer, Alex Papworth, Frank Pascal, Anesh Patel, Husain Patel, Monali Patel, Sarah Patterson, Emily Patton, Kelly Payne, Melanie Pearson, Maria Penella Gomez, Adele Pentland, Laura Perez Marino, Gayle Peskett, Tanya Pile, Cezar Pineda Jr, Simon Prag, Jessica Prangnell, David Pratt, Marcellina Priadi, Angela Prince, Bathoni Puplampu, Raska Radulovic, Luis Ramos Villegas, Cristina Rapacioli, Rosie Riley, Stephen Riley, Sonja Ristic, Ian Robinson, Amber Rocke, Jodie Rodaway, Noelia Rufete-Gil, Warren Rushton, Matthew Sabourin, Laura Sage, Vanessa Samafu, Harminder Sandhu, Mara Sandres, Emma Savory, Anieka Saxby, Andy Scott, Adam Seaman, Tanya Seymour, Robert Shand, Ray Shenholds, Leonie Shephard, Amy Shepherd, Robyn Sherwell, Quentin Silvand, Lewis Simington, Jen Sims, Angeline Smith, Laura-Anne Smith, Nadia Sotiropoulos, Josie Sparkes, Louise Stagg, Anna-Maria Stavrakellis, Rhea Stennett, Suzanne Stone, Tischa Stossler, Eirian Stovell, Stanislav Tarasovs, Stephanie Tavernier, James Taylor, Mia Taylor, Abbi Tew, Elvira Thissen, Fay Thomas, Amy Thomas, Tayla Thomas, Shimelle Thornbury, Michael Torres, Ellen Travers, Juan Tu, Gigi Tuazon, Emily Tully, Emma Turner, Clare Uchima, Mani Upadhyaya, Nicola Varley, Marit Vestby, Noorin Virani, Anthony Vodden, Samar Wafa, Erin Wagner, Graham Waite, Jacqueline Waite, Tam Walton, Jimmy Waters, Alice Watts, Edward Weaver, Mia Webb, Amy Welch, Chris Weston-Simons, Hannah White, Russell White, Katie Wilcock, Vicki Willatts, Karl Willett, Emma Williams, Laura Williams, Grace Willis-Hodgins, Sarah Withers, Angela Wood, Matt Woodgate, Rachel Worley, Ashley Wright, Ricky Zalman, Nika Zelinska **Street Party** Daniel Abreu Mendoza, Donald Adaakwah, Will Aitchison, Shanead Akyena, Alvi Alam, Val Alderton, Nathifa Alexander, Clive Amos, Karen Appleby, Alar Arge, David Armer, Amelia Armstrong, Rachel Asante, Lucy Ashall, Curtis Ashley, Paul Atherton, Perry Atkins, Ifemide Atunwa, Dominyka Aurylaite, Jesutoni Awoseyi, Ollie Ayling, John Backwell, Chris Badrick, Mohammad Bajwa, Blayne Baker, Peter Baker, Marien Balla, Abigail Bamsey, Jennifer Barlow, Sophie Barnes, Shyann Barrett, Jay Batchelor, Jenna Bayliss, Karen Bell, Ray Bennett, Dom Betts, Neil Beveridge, Harry Biddle, Abdullah Bin Moklisur Rahman, Molly Birch, Palma Black, Charles Blackshaw, Dianne Bluston, Frimpong Boateng, Ben Boatman, Michaela Boller, Andy Boot, Charlotte Boulton, Laurence Anne Bouvard, Penny Branch, Nicholas Brand, Chris Brice, Amy Briggs, Ross Burnett, Adam Buteux, Jacob Butler, Sheila Caden, Megan Callen, Sean Canning, Teresa Carlile, John David Carrion, Ian Carroll, Rachael Carter-Eagleton, Thomas Caton, Jacky Chan, Lewis Chapman, Jonathan Chase, Balraj Chatha, Labib Ahmed Choudhury, Luke Christodoulou, Lorraine Clark, Oliver Clayton, Jamie Cole, Melody Cole, Leonardo Collazos Moran, Karole Conroy, Caroline Constable, Adam Cook, Joe Cook, Lyn Cook, Raymond Coombs, Daniel Cooper, Richard Cooper, Liz Cordingley, Kelsey Cornell, Tommy Covington Young, Isabelle Cox, Mary Cox, Philip Cox, Rich Cristina, Megan Crudgington, Georgie Curd, Chris Curley, Bruce Currie, Ed Curry, Taylor Dallas, Christine Davis, Grace Davis, Warren Davis, Madelaine Denoon, Sanheeta Dighé, Zoe Dines, Kai Dodson, Murat Dogan, Roger Drew, Eugene Dugan, Alison Duncan, Faye Durkin, Pete Dyson, Billy Ebanks, Jessica Egoh, Robert Eldridge, Keith Elliott, Shannon Emerson, Sarag England, Malcolm Ennin, Jessica Etherden, Karen Lague, Laura Evans, Eva Farace, Nigel Farmer, Gemma Fawsitt, Shegs Fayase, Taylor Fern, Susan Finch, Salamatu Fofanah, Ben Frances, Melanie Franklin, Joshua Fredericks, Sam Freer, Jordan Gallimore, Bobbie Gargrave, Kyriana Georgiou Delisle, Maram Ghirri, Steve Gibbs, Ella Gibson, Angela Gilkes, Gurpal Gill, Adam Gillam, Megan Gillard, Victoria Gladden, Matthew Goodwin, Fiona Goodwin, Bill Graham, Claire Grant, Louise Gray, Richard Green, Andrew Green, Laura Green, Thomas Green, Andrew Greer, Duncan Greig, Jonathan Griffiths, Natasha Hale, Peter Hall, Benjamin Hammersley, Charles Harden, Lynn Harmer, John Harrington, Justine Harris, Danielle Harris, Kirsty Harris, Morenike Harrison-Obafemi, Ian Hart, Erin Harvey, Deborah Hassan, Dylan Haughton, Suraiya Hawa, Jörg Heinen, Gill Hepburn, Damien Hewitt, Vic Hibbert, Katherine Hicks, Alex Highfield, Mary Hill, Sharon Hoadley, David Hodgson, Demi-May Hoffman, Jackie Holloway, Chloe Horrell, Gary Horsman, Steve Howard, Peter Howes, Jenny Hughes, Christopher Humphries, Pamela Jacques, Ashley Jarvest, Ting Jiang, Sandy Johnston, Alan Jones, Ben Jones, Chris Jones, Nigel Jordan, Nicholas Hardy, Samanta Jurasiute, Lynne Kahr, Mahtab Kailey, James Kane, Beata Karolyi, Richard Keane, John Kearney, Micky Keel, Nicole Keeping, Andrew Kennedy, Phil Kennedy, Justine Kerry, Louise Kershaw, Mary Keys, Muhammad Khalid, Maureen Khamjani, Tracy Knight, Komal Komalpreet Panasar, Lukas Kondzeliauskas, Finney Koshy, Prince Kosoko, Electra Kotopouli, Diana Kryuyy, Koby Kulater, Harmesh Kumar, Joanne Laurent, Lynn Leathem, Gay Leggett, Jessie Leong, Boyan Levchev, Julian Lewis, Vivienne Linton, Colin Little, Kelly Lock, Michael Loiacono, Rosaire Longelo, Hilary Lowe, Jordan Lowe, Maya Luu, Terry Lynch, Chris Magdziarz, Gaynor Maher, Dahni Maisuria, Joy Maitland, Joseph Maksymowicz, Kellie Malone, Filipina Manuel, Nick Marsden, Ian Martin, Claire Massey, Calvinder Mattoo, Ellen Maulkerson, Adem Mazreku, Meta-Keina Mbayo, Brian Mcaleese, Callum Mcclusky, Walter Mcculloch, Chloe Mcdonald, Ryan Mcguire, Edisa Meha, Arif Meherali, Victoria Mellard, Arman Memarzadeh, Grace Merry, Mary Messer, Danusia Michalik, Jeanette Miller, Jason Millington, Jon Moll, Lesley Montague, Ruth Montlake, Anna Moody, Derek Moore, Roland Moore, Billy Morahan, Norma Morgan, Rachel Morley, Charlotte Morris, Gemma Morris, Debbie Morton, Hanani Mukendi, Richard Murray, Lee Newport, Benjamin Pfeiffer-Key, James Norton, Sian Notley, Jake Nurdin, Roslyn O'Garro, Charissa Ogundijo-Akinfenwa, Karl O'Keeffe, Devine Okoli, Otto Okun, Elizabeth Olafioye, Adrian Oldershaw, Davis Olupitam, Muhammed Omarjee, Victoria Onwukwe Wilson, Fiona Orford-Williams, Aimee Orwell, Elen Paloots, Amar Panesar, Amita Parikh, Jeremy Parker, Andy Parr, Katie Paul, Tom Paul, Amy Pearce, Janet Pendrey, Aydin Phillips, Sonia Phillips, William Phillips, Mason Pidgeon, Jon Pierce, Wendy Pierce, David Plummer, Fiona Porritt, Gary Power, Thomas Powis, Aleasha Price, Jan Prince, Stephen Prosser, Zane Pupola, Chen Qian, Duncan Ramsey, Christopher Randall, Nicholas Read-Lord, Billy Reynolds, Dylan Reynolds, Lucina Ridgwell, Oliver Rimoldi, Sarah Riordan, Joanna Risolino, Brett Robinson, Alan Robinson, Charlie Rose, Sonja Rose, Adam Roux, Dominic Rowntree, Laraine Ruddy, Jonathan Rudge, Christopher Saban, William Sach, Shannon Saise-Marshall, Alicia Salami, Dean Salter, Stephanie Sampson, Danielle Samuel, Neha Sanakal, Stéphane Schneider, Kimberley Schultz, Kathleen Secker, Keiron Senyah, Claudia Sermbezis, Judy Shakespeare, Ikraam Sharif, Bartley Shaw, Kirstie Shaw, Luana Silva, Devon Simmans, Michael Simmons, Roger Simpson, Arun Sivarajah, Armandas Smailys, Rebecca Smith, Garry Smith, Lewis Smith, Oladapo Smith, Lisa Somerville, Geetha Sooriyacumar, Jean Sowden, Harriet Spoor, Karen Steel, Emily Stepaniuk, Natasha Stewart, David Stokes, Sarah Stopforth, Koichiro Sugimori, Lax Sundavadra, Maureen Sydric, Csilla Szeles, David Taylor, Yuriko Teer, Victoria Thain, Jack Thompson, Joanna Tickner, Andy Tomkinson, Ian Torres, Claire Tremeer, Malcolm Trice, Bob Trimble, Karen Tull, Geoff Unwin, Coen Van Der Zanden, Kishor Vara, Georgia Vaughan, Marcela Vicente, Daniel Voss, Jamie Wagstaff, Doreen Walford, Lynn Warner, Justin Watkins, Gerogie-Lee Wedge, Alex Westcott, Sasha Whaley, Michael White, Christopher Whitehead, Paul Wiffen, Connie Williams, Nicole Willis, Charles Wilson, Tim Woolley, Amy Wright, Mona Felicia Zaw, Qian Zhang, Paula Zwaap **Waterloo Sunset** Mohammed Sahib Abdul, Tolu Abisogun, Judith Ackaa, Emmanuel Addo, Miracle Adebanjo, Mehvish Afzal, Kaede Agyemang, Tina Ahang, Fahad Ahmed, Yasin Ahmed, Naveen Ahmed, Aleya Akhtar, Nazia Akthar, Shama Akther, Christopher Alabi, Alfie Alburey, Julia Alija, Lejla Alija, Abbie Allen, Ingana Almada, Leila Aminul, Amaad Amjad, Muhammad Amjad, Rachel Anderson, Tyrell Andrew, Julia Antoniewska, Nana Appiah, Damilola Araba, Esmee Arnold, Edith Attridge, Mohammed Awan, Rudeyna Awas, Tuhin Aziz, Oumme Badul, Harry Bailey, Marcella Bailey, Jacob Baines-Vosper, Alanna Baker, Georgia Baker, Molly Baker, Vienna Barnes, Jean Barnett, Michael Barnett, Connor Bartlett, Ryan Bartlett, Henrik Bassett, Jane Bassett, Shannon Bassett, Collin Batte, Hannah Baughn, Isaac Beck, Nicole Beeson, Aysha Begum, Gabriela Benedetti, Charlie Benjamin, Blaine Bennetts, Paul Besgrove, Ruth Bidgood, Shannon Biggins, Shelby Black, Sasha Bonner, Barbara Bouman, Georgia Bowers, Dean Bowman, Aaron Bradley-Shankar, Neamh Breen, Ramone Brown, Adam Buckingham, Jacob Bukasa, Luke Burton, Joanna Byrne, Melanie Cahuasqui, Amber Campbell-White, Amelia Cappi, Naomi Cardoso, Mia Carroll, Shona Carter, Sarah Caseley, Anjana Chandegra, Frankie Chapman, Rozlind Chapman, Junia Charlton, Magdalena Charlwood, Katerine Chauca Chavez, Inshirah Chaudhry, Harjinder Chauhan, Dylan Chellng, Emma Chika, Samiya Chowdhury, Lee Diep Chu, Tegan Churchill, Lucy Cientanni, Sally Jayne Cockburn, Caroline Cogbill, Kobina Coker, Michael Collins, Alice Connolly-Taylor, Camila Consolmagno, Daniel Cook, Mark Coombs, Leighanne Cowler, Laura Cox, Stephen Crawford, Cheryl Crombie, Isabell Cromwell, Ellis Cunningham, Kathryn Daniels, Savannah Davamolas, Eve Davidson, Mark Davies, Victoria Davis, Michelle Dedman, Nethanie Delmas, Jerome Demart, Georgia Demmon, Aqkella Denny, Anna Devlin, Iole Dexter, Amanveer Dhanjal, Grace Dick-Oakley, Jessie Dike, Ruby Dollner, Tommy Downey, Edmond Duda, Izichiokike Elenwo, Jake Ellis Price, Casey Ely, Ruby Evans, Michelle Faber, Lewis Falconer, Jamie Faulkner, Jamil Ferdaws, Mandy Ferguson, Islam Fessih, Sinead Firman, Nathalie Fitzgerald, Joss Foot, Douglas Fordyce, Eleanor Franks, Lukenny Freire Tinta, Paul Frempong, Anne Gammon, Katie Garcia, Megan Garraghan, Laure Garrard, Paul Gellard, Rasida Gerald, Farkhondeh

Volunteers
Bénévoles

Ghairat, Brenda Gill, Montgomery Gordon, Alun Gordon, Quilan Greaves, Kika Green, Emma Greene, Andrew Griffiths, Neil Griffiths, Scarlet Griffiths, Frances Groves, Adedoyinsola Haastrup, Natalie Haggis, Abdul-Kareem Haji, Max Hales, Nicola Hales-Jepp, Skye Halsey, Alfred Hammond, Kalesha Hanson, Ishika Haque, Beverley Jane Harris, Cannon Harrison, Kate Hawkins, Joshua Hayes, Annette Henry, Lauren Hill, Bryn Holder, Joseph Housham-Whitby, Niazi Houssein, Dean Howard, Devante Hudson, Tracy Hughes, Libaan Hussein, Natalie Iino Hayes, Nicholas Illingworth, Robin Inyat, Taylar Isaac, Juhedul Islam, Kifayat Islam, Ifenna Izuchukwu, Manisha Jadeja, Ronan James, Callum Jenkin, Devina John-Lewis, Rhea Johnson, Yewande Johnson, Amy Jones, Armanie Jones, Hector Jones, Pat Jones, Juanita Justus, Bhajan Kalsi, James Karageorgis, Axiana Kasanganay, Jade Kelly, Jonathan Kelly, Carl Kemp, Lauren Kemp, Maheen Khan, Zain Khan, Zairah Khan, Nadirah Khan, Farzana Khatun, Jade Kirk, Ewan Kirton, Jason Kizomba, Maureen Koim, Georgi Kostov, Leon La, Brandon Lakeman, Diya Lakhani, Michelle Lamptey, Georgia Lancaster, Andre Lavinier, Sara Lawlor, Conor Lawton, Rhea Lempert, Ashley Lewis, Joshua Lewis, Gabriel Licka, Tyla Lord-Stamp, Mark Lotter, Angela Louka, Maria Lubbe, Jesy Luyengi, Andrew Mackenzie, Amy Mackenzie, Filicia Malins, Dinis Manuel, Siobhan Martin, Chelsea Mather, Lukas Matlasaitis, Jillian Matovu, Elise Matthews, Nathan Mbelevuidi, Adam Mcassey, Cameron Mccarthy, Micah McDowell, Bailey Mcewen, Caroline Mcintyre, Philip Mcintyre, Gabriella Mckay-Jones, Eduard Meha, Emel Mehmet, Adam Mehmood, Ankar Miah, Nizam Miah, Gilbert Miller, Aaron Miller Anderson, Mohamed Mohamed, Nadia Mohammed, Thabang Mokori, Jessie Moore, Sean Moore, Esra Mor, Paige Morgan, Ellen Morley, Casey Morrison , Tapuwa Mushanduri, Tyler Nagar, Sakeena Naqvi-Jukes, Phillip Nathan, Eunice Neto, Jemima Neto, Abbie Newton, Sarah Nicklin, Tahera Noor, Famida Noor Mohomed, Chuka Nwanodi-Chikaanya, Rose Nye, Heather Odd, Simon Odd, Andre O'Garro, Taiwo Ogunbiyi, Yvonne O'Keeffe-Mol, Oluwatobiloba Oluyede, Oyinkan Onajinrin, Mekala Oxley, Piotr Ozgur, Christopher Palmer, Joyce Pascal, Aqil Patel, Atif Patel, Vishal Hitesh Patel, Annie Payne, Linda Peppiatt, Thomas Phillips, Lola Phillips-Leal, Annie Phipps, Berfin Pirbudak, Andrew Pountain, Natalie Premru, Bailey Pryce, Thomas Quigg, Maria Quinlan, Mikon Rahman, Abigail Ralph, Charlie Ramm, Neena Ranchod-Shaw, Davina Rattanpal, Egzon Rexha, Marc Riley, Bruce Roberts, Eugenie Robinson Lee, Gregory Rodwell, Mark Rogers, Christopher Rogers, Keri Rothwell-Douglas, Elinor Rowe, Hannah Roy-Davies, Shana Runglall, Carys Russell, Scarlett Russell, Shanara Sadeque, Aminat Salau, Adam Saleh, Mohammed Sami, Terryanne Saunders, Conor Sawenko, Olivia Scher, Vinith Selvanathan, Bikash Sen, Harry Sewell, Luke Sewell, Nawaz Shanvari, Richard Shields, Hamza Siddiqui, Billy Siequien, Melissa Sindrey, Sukhraj Singh, Louis Small, Dominic Smith, Laura Smith, Natalie Smith, Stanley Smith, Thomas Smith, Jackson Snell, Melisande Soares Lopes, Dawid Sobierajski, Izabella Sozal, Millie Spalding, Poppy Spalding, Lily Standing, Jaden Stephenson, Carol Stevens, Paige Stone, Jonathan Stranks, Justine Suba, Braida Sumgo Zola, Monsurat Sunmonu, Mario Svetiev, Perise Swaray-Agbloe, Aaisha Syed, Sharon Talbot, Lucinda Tandon, Adedamilola Tariuwa, Charlie Tate, Pamela Taupaj, Isabelle Taylor, Rory Thompson, Poppy Tollemache, Daniel Tolley, Dilara Tufa, Nicholas Turner, Tegan Turton, Imrana Uddin, Jabir Uddin, Eliza Ullersperger, Nazia Umme, Adam Upcott, Alice Upcott, Edward Upcott, Alexander Uttley, Irena Vajagic, Ella Vaughan, Amrit Virdee, Gurvinder Virdee, Simran Virdee, Isabella Vogel, Sindy Wade, Tanvir Wadud, Daniel Waite, Liliana Walduck, Megan Warde, Cheynne Waters, Caroline Watkins, Jada Watkiss, Natalie Watson, Lewis Watts, Elizabeth Welch, Kerri West, Chymaya White, Kyra White, Tina Whitehead, Kate Williams, Violet Williams, Jayden Williams-Mayer, Gareth Wood, George Wood, Hollianne Wood, Annmarie Woodcraft, Wendy Woodroof, Kirsty Wrighton, Mairi Ottilie Wyatt Gosebruch, Imran Yacoob, Nicola Yellop, Morton Yesufu, Mohamed Yunis, Ahmed Zen **One Day Like This** Derek Abbey, Ian Abbott, Laura Abbott, Lynsey Abernethy, Joyce Abosi, Adejoke Abudu, Jane Adams, Nell Adams, Mosun Adebayo, Elizabeth Adediran, Elizabeth Adlington, Otibho Agbareh, Angela Agyei, Des Agyekumhene, Marcus Aitman, Adeola Akitoye, Imad Al Dakkak, Blessing Aladetoun, Rafiqul Alam, Javier Albarracin Perea, Alister Albert, Charles Albert, Kelly Al-Dakkak, Charlotte Aldhouse, Holly Alexander, Jim Allen, Jonny Allen, Camille Alleyne, Laura Alleyne, Samantha Alleyne, Amonn Al-Mahrouq, Zahra Amlani, Beverley Amoah, Lisa Anderson, Thomas Andrews, Karl Anns, Gerard Antony, Amy Anzel, Veronica Apolinario, Charlotte Appleby, Lucy Appleton, Dejaar Arabshahi Fard, Baven Arasaretnam, Ricardo Araujo, Kathleen Arbuckle, Emma Arden, June Arinze, Toni Armiger, Amanda Arnold, Samuele Aru, Khelisyah Ashamu, Ewan Ashburn, Ian Ashby, Thomas Ashcroft-Nowicki, Mandy Ashmore, Gina Atherton, Lola Atkins-Omojola, Usharani Augstine, Subash Bacheta, William Badham, Kirsty Baffour, Stephen Baines, Tejvir Bains, Niha Bajpai, Alexandra Baker, Cheryl Baker, Emily Baker, Vicki Baldwin, Liz Ball, Olivia Ball, Steve Ball, Haiko Ballieux, Bernie Bane, Eva Banik, Susan Banks, Laura Baranik, Amrit Barard, Karen Baratram, Martyn Barber, Guna Bareika, Jennie Barham, Tuahid Barik, Matthew Barnes, Denise Barr, James Barr, Susan Barr, Natalie Barrett, Kieran Bartlett, Jo Barton, Sally Barton, Samsrithaa Baskaran, Corinne Bass, Mikaela Bates, Tristan Baylis, Anthony Bealing, Kat Beaty, Khiltee Beeharry, Poppy Begum, Cathryn Bell, Rashidat Bello, David Belnick, Ugne Bendikaite, Volodymyr Bendikov, Conrad Benjamin, Gillian Bennet, James Bennett, James Benwell, Adam Berry, Melissa Bethune, Katrina Betteridge, Valeria Bettini, John Beveney, Tim Beveridge, Harpreet Bhal, Jasmeet Bhambra, Jamie Biddle, Gary Biggs, Kate Binchy, Jean Bincliffe, Alice Bird, James Bird, Katie Birmingham, Dav Bisessar, Emily Bishop, Briony Black, Alan Blackmore, Nathaniel Blake, Rob Blakemore, Emma Blamey, Adam Joseph Bloomfield, Chris Bloomfield, Thomas Bloomfield, Darren Boakye-Adjei, Margaret Boden, Paro Bodini, Jemma Bogan, Nadine Bogan, Sylvie Bolioli, Helen Bond, Jenn Botterill, Fatima Boudafcha, Adrian Bouillin, Natasha Boult, David Bower, Fredrica Bowkett, Ian Boyd, Becky Brass, Philip Bremang, Laura Brennan, Simon Brett, Rachel Brewer, Cathrine Bright, James Bright, Tristan Bright, David Brighton, Hollie Brill, Jayson Brinkler, Nigel Brinklow, Joe Brookman, Jonathan Brooks, Laura Brooks, Ben Brown, Cathy Brown, Karen Brown, Kat Brown, Katherine Brown, Lennox Brown, Louise Brown, Scott Brown, Susan Brown, Deborah Bryant, Kathy Buley, Larissa Bulla, Alice Bullard, Fiona Bullard, Clare Bullen, Caroline Bunker, Sally Bunker, Paul Burne, Penny Burrows, Sophie Burrows, Kellie Butcher, Michael Cafferkey, Stefan Caiafa, Alex Callaghan, Marie Calvert, Melanie Cameron, Hollie Campbell, Megan Campbell, Sean Campbell-Hynes, Vikki Canniford, Carol Carr, Eliene Santana Carreiro , John Carstairs, Anne-Marie Carter, Diogo Carvalho, Rebecca Carver, Darryl Causon, Joanna Cavan, Louise Cave, Valeria Cazas, Lun Chai, Rebecca Chamberlain, Sylvia Chan, Darius Chatfield, John Chatfield, Kakia Chatsiou, Tarun Chavda, Raj Rani Chawla, Donald Chen, Robert Cherry, Suet Yee Cheung, Nick Childs, Chiutsu Chiutsu, Beverly Christie, Sandy Chui, Trevor Church, Rosa Cisneros, Charles Clark, Elaine Clark, Hugh Clark, James Clark, Nick Clark, Christine Cleaver, Marion Close, David Coatesworth, Siobhan Cockfield, Christina Coker, Jonathan Cole, Mariatu Cole, Nicola Coles, Chris Collier, Lynn Collier, Eki Connolly, Roseanna Connolly, Amelia Cook, Stephen Cook, Matthew Cooksey, Simon Cooksey, Lisa Coomey, Natalie Cooper, Andrew Copley, Josie Coster, Marie-Caroline Cotel, Amy Jane Cotter, Alistair Cowan, Anthony Cowan, Janine Cowie, Annette Cox, Colin Coxall, Rebecca Coxon, Philippa Cradock, Ross Craib, Steven Crane, Julia Crawley-Boevey, Alec Creed, Terrie Creswell, Rhona Crewe, Blair Crichton, David Crick, Suzanne Cross, Gillian Crow, Victoria Custerson, Vena Dacent, Irina Danilova, Susmita Das, Catherine Davies, Peter Davies, Toby Davies, David Davis, Kathy Davison, William Davison, Hayley Dawson, Alexandre Yemaoua Dayo, Kim De Ram, Pedro De Sousa, Helen Dear, Alesha De-Freitas, Elizabeth Demetriou, Emma Dengate, Danielle Deveney, Ruth Dewdney, Parveen Dhanda, Mani Dhani, Rimini Dick-Carr, Guy Dickens, Hannah Diribe, Isobel Dobson, Jessykar Donald, Xianhui Dong, Carl Donoghue, Liza Dos Santos, Maria Dos Santos Veiga, Sue Douglass, Dmitry Drozdov, Miriam Dubois, Maria Emilia Dutto, Nicola Dykes, Vicki Eddens, Michelle Edney, Rebecca Edwards, Leila Elbahy, Penny Elkins, Nicola Elliott, Selina Elliott, Chris Ellis, Erica Emm, Crystal Emmanuel, Anna Eriksson, Giles Ernsting, Taiwo Eshinlokun, Rahim Esmail, Louise Etheridge, Russell Eubanks, Jim Evans, Katie Evans, Mark Evans, Rachel Evans, Lauren Eve, Zuza Fabiszak, Remi Fadare, Felipe Fagundes, Marcos Fagundes, Richard Fairs, Yuan Fang, Margaret Farmiloe, Melanie Farquharson, Adele Fash, Martine Faulkner, Carol Felts, Rocio Fernandez Fresquet, Denis Fernando, Fernando Ferreira Dos Santos, Rebekah Fielding-Haynes, Ellen Fife, David Figg, Caroline Firman, Caroline Fisher, Sarah Fisher, Simon Fisher, Martin Fitzgerald, Preston Fitzgerald, Katherine Fodor, Michelle Forde, Bray Foster, Cru Fox, Hugh Fox, Sue Foyle, Jennifer Franich, Miriam Franz, Emma Frayne, Shaun Freeman, Jonathan French, Robert Frost, Dancemastergozi Fulani, Sean Fullerton, Polly Fung, Lorraine Furneaux, Henry Fynn, Christian Gabriel, Jemima Gaddam, Charlie Galarza, Emma Gale, Christian Gangeri, Fei Gao, Charlotte Garey, Lucia Gavalova, Amanda-Jane Geddes, Lara Gee, Thomas Gell, Tina Gellie, Cally Gentle, Jackie Gentle, Simon Gentry, Monique Geraghty, Jagjit Gidda, Kieran Giffen, Howard Gilbert, Joy Grace Gilbert, Alice Gilkes, Jennifer Gilkes, Adrian Gill, Gilly Gilmour, Luke Girvan, Shaz Gitay, Tim Goddard, Suzanne Goldberg, John Gomez, Leo Gonzalez, Charlotte Goodhew, Dan Goodhind, Olivia Gooding, Stewart Goshawk, Lydia Gosnell Dougan, Joanie Goss, Keef Gould, Marilyn Gould, Neil Goulder, Raju Govindasamy Muthuswamy, Aimee Goyette, Bruce Graham, Eric Grainger, John Grant, Andy Gray, Julius Gray, Charlotte Green, Matthew Green, Elisabeth Greenbank, Roberta Greenhalgh, Kim Griffiths, Lynda Griffiths, Laura Grist, Xiaofei Gui, Yan Guo, Kiran Guraya, Abigail Gurr, Keiji Gurung, Jo Gweshe, Elsa Gwilliam, Lisa Ha, Peter Hackmann, Loretta Hadjikoumi, Nick Hafezi, Nicola Haji-Antonis, Stef Hale, Rebecca Hales, Clare Halifax, Alison Hall, Joey Hall, Phill Hall, Maria Hamalainen, Edward Han, Flo Hanson, Ornella Hardie, Daniel Harding, Phil Hardisty, James Hargreaves, Anjali Hariharan, Melanie Harper, Bridget Harrison, Gideon Hart, Ben Hartley, Kate Harvey, Amina Hassam Hassam, Peter Hawker, Catherine Hawkes, Victoria Hawkes, Amanda Hawthorne, Andrew Hawtin, Kevin Haycock, Caryn Haynes, Ben Hayter, Patsy Hayward, Dominic Hayward-Peel, Tim Hearn, Alex Henderson, Anne Henwood, Leticia Alejandra Herrera Perez, Cristina Heselden, Jonathan Hewett, Ailsa Hewitt, Kathleen Hicks, Karl Hildebrandt, Nicola Hill, Sara Hill, Louise Hilliard, Catherine Hillis, Kirsty Hinchliff, Felicity Hindle, Rich Hinwood, Graham Hirst, Naomi Hiscock, Martin Hissey, Stephanie Hitchins, Sarah Hixson, Wendy Ho, Juliet Hogarth, Nicola Hogg, Emma Holden, Laura Hollands, Zoe Holloway, Catrina Holmes, Matthew Holmes, Lewis Holt-Brown, Bhupinder Hoonjan, Christine Hopson, Ildi Horvath, Helen Hosking, Christine Houghton, Edward Howard, Howell Howell, Max Hoy, Michal Hrncir, Wan-Ting Hsieh, Huarui Huang, Jane Huang, Katrina Hughes, Charlie Huins, Nathan Humphreys, Polly Hunt, Drew-Levi Huntsman, Paul Hurford, Josue Hurtado, Adnan Hussain, Akthar Hussain, Joshua Hustwick, Tina Ilsley, Haider Ilyas, Inemesit Imoh, Mary Impey, Vicky Instone, Cyrus Iravani, Robert Irving, Victoria Irving, Helen Isaacs, Nurul Islam, Helen Ives, Claire Jackson, Felicity Jackson, Tiffany Jackson, Cristiane Jacobs, Manish Jagatiya, Paul James, Stephen James-Yeoman, Stuart Janes, Isobel Jayawardane, Suzie Jeeves, Megha Jhaveri, Jingyuan Jiang, John John, Joely Johnson, Sheree Johnson, Larry Johnson, Vanessa Johnson, Mark Johnson-Brown, Andrew Johnston, Alexander Jones, Allan Jones, Caris Jones, Charles Jones, Helena Jones, Jenn Jones, Matthew Jones, Beverley Jordan, Christine Josef-Santos, Roshini Joseph, Sandra Joseph, Madhuri Joshi, Mukesh Joshi, Nikita Joshi, Helen Jousselin, Vinay Kabra, Lilly Kambo, Maulik Kamdar, Millie Karn, Carla Kaspar, Grainne Kavanagh, Brian Kavanagh, Romany Kebar, John Keech, Hana Kelblova, Neil Kelsey, Peter Keltie, Alastair Kember, Howard Kemp, Lindsay Kennedy, Jenny Kent, Katherine Kent, Peter Kenyon, Claudia Keston, Catherine Ketsimur, Sam Key, Frances Keyton, Pareena Khairdin, Liudmila Khvan, Kibue-Ngare Kibue, Lyndsey Kilkenny, Yerrie Kim, Blair King, Kirsten King, Warren King, Cassie Kingston, Angela Kiss, Tim Kiss Freitas, Andrea Kitzberger, Elizabeth Kliman, Lesley Knight, Eve Knights, Deborah Knox-Hewson, Zoltan Komlosi, Liane Kordan, Helen Kowald, Luisa Krampoutsa, Lukas Krohn-Grimberghe, Siva Kumaravel, Yvonne Kumi, Alexandre Kündig, Alexander Kustow, Margaret Labongo, Peter Laemmle, Miles Lampitt, Clare Lane, Cathryn Langdon, Danny Langston, Jayne Larnie, Erika Laszlo, Hong-Tin Lau, Ade Lawless, Maria Lawrence, Jan Lawry, Laura Lawson, Samantha Lawson, Constance Lawton, Dea Le Bargy, Emmanuelle Le Drian, Kieran Leahy, Victoria Lebor, Bethan Lee, Le Kai Lee, Danyang Lei, Viktoria Lengyel, Nicholas Lennon, Oliver Leonard, Jessica Leung, Angela Lewis, Desmond Lewis, Kristina Lewis, Leonie Lewis, Lewis Lewis, Mark Lewis, Michael Lewis, Naomi Lewis, Shuang Li, Ying Li, Yunlu Li, Bo Li-Bean, Elsa Lignos, Zhen Lim, Wendy Lim, Ming Lin, John Lines, James Lister, Jianning Liu, Hannah Lloyd-Jones, Bradley Lloyd-Prest, David Lockwood, Keith Lockwood, Dave Longman, Michael Longridge, Vicky Lord, Katie Louch, Derek Love, Sarah Lowes, Dominic Lown, Xialan Lu, Adam Lucas, Angela Lucas, Robert Lucas, Flo Lunt, Xiaomin Luo, Michaela Lupton, Hugh Macpherson, Peter Magee, Sophie Maggs, Deborah Magri-Overend, Shaun Maguire, Corinne Maillet, Jock Maitland, Stefan Majczak, Paras Malde, Sepehr Malekahmadi, Mary Ann Mangano, Kayleigh Mann, Darren Marash, Roman Marie, Cassandra Marillier, Tracey Marshall, Lynda Martin, Wendy Martin, Alistair Matson, Mutsumi Matsuba, Ellie Matthews, Melissa Matthews, Sally Maxwell, Rachel Mayes, Sarah Mccaffrey, Judeth Mccall, Matthew Mccourt, Charmaine Mccracken, Paul Mccrudden, Ewan Mcdonald, Natalie Mcgrath, Rowlands Mchale, Hugh Mclaren, Katherine Mclean, Robert Mead, Gemma Mears, Roopal Mehta, Giuseppe Membrino, Shauna Mennis, Seema Menon, Leandro Mariano Mera Otero, Jane Michele, Anna Miles, Ben Milway, Caroline Mistry, Raj Mistry, Kurt James Mitchell, Aye Moe, Ahmed Mohideen, George Monisse, Annabelle Monks, Hannah Montrose, Jack Moody, Simon Mooney, Kevin Moore, Daniel Moravanszky, Rebecca Morgan, Alex Morgan, Liz Morgan, Sonia Morjaria, Katie Morris, Reanne Morris, Tim Morrish, Anya Morrison, Rachel Moses, Sarah Moss, Celia Moutell, Ann Moyse, Marcus Mozley, Laura Muir, Sarah Mujinya-Motima, Shirley Mukisa, Babita Mundra, Jim Munro, Francesca Muro, Claire Murphy, Murphy Murphy, Philippa Murray, Christina Myers, Zoltan Nagy, Rosemin Najmudin, Angela Nascimento, Aseem Natekar, Nila Natkunan, Eileen Naughton, Beverley Nderu, Russell Neal, Tom Needham, Sonia Nelson-Williams, Caroline Nembharde, Tim Neumann, Tim Newbould, Annabel Newell, Ross Newsome, Veronica Newson, Ellis Ngui, Margaret Ngui, Sabine Nguini, Susan Nguyen, Beth Nguyen, Charlotte Nice, Katie Nicholas, Lauren Nickless, Mauro Niewolski, John Nixon, Danica Noh, Craig Nolan, Carolyn Norgate, Inderjeet Notta, Deirdre Nugent, Stephen Nunn, Aileen Nurse, Kariba Nwodo, Will Oakey, Mirian Obiozo, Sarah O'Brien, Brendan O'Connor, Stuart O'Dell, Caroline Odogwu Odogwu, Steve O'Gallagher, Bernadene Ogle, Patricia Olabre, Suliet Oladokun, Tomasz Olejniczak, Hugo Oliveira, Charlene Oliver, Diana Olloova, Saira O'Mallie, Sarah Ong, Lizzy Orcutt, Graham Orriss, Juan Ortiz Fernandez, Kima Otung, Robert Owen, Nicky Owen, Cemile Ozkan, Verinder Pardesi, Lisa Parfitt, Pauline Park, Claire Parker, Edward Parker, Caitlin Parr, Deb Parsons, Matt Parsons, Rupal Patel, Padmraj Patil, James Paton, Adrian Pavia, Andy Pawsey, James Peach, Malcolm Peake, Jan Pearson, Dave Peirson, Hanna Peltonen, Natalie Pereech, Charlotte Pereira, Randolph Pereira, David Perkins, Jen Perkins, Ann Persson, Tom Peters, Vivien Peters, Theresa Peterson, Kathy Petrakis, Katrina Pett, Christopher Peugniez, Dominic Pflaum, Daniel Pharaoh, Sunanta Phattanavibul, Aisha Phipps, James Pickford, Rebecca Pike, Rolando Pincay Macias, Jessica Pinho, Jonathan Fabian Pinho, Monica Piovesana, Sam Pitt, Milana Plecas, Lukian Poleschtschuk, Deborah Pollard, Anja Pomeroy, Sarah Pope, Louise Port, Simon Porter, Tabitha Porter, Anna Portosi, Vivienne Potter, Hannah Powell, Zoe Prag, Alistair Prestidge, Paula Preston, Jess Price, Steve Price, Lynnette Prigmore, Tiffany Pritchard, Tom Pritchard, Katie Proctor, Liva Puce, Gill Purnell, Gemma Putney, Sam Pye, Zhaoyu Qi, Janeen Quentin, Hannah Quigley, Brendan Quinn, Sarah Radcliffe, Michel Radermecker, Izzie Radley, Sonia Rafferty, Faizur Rahman, Avnish Raichura, Sonia Raichura, Thara Raj, Shamma Rajan, Rashmi Rajyaguru, Ruby Rall, Vanessa Ralte, Sinead Rampat, Michelle Ramrachia, Clare Ramsaran, Lindsay Ramsbottom, Preeti Rana, James Randall, David Rapp, Sarah Ratford, Kumaran Ravendradas, Darryl Rayner, Kayley Redrup, David Rees, Luke Reeve, Anya Reevell, Olivia Reevell, Jo Regis, Lisiane Reis Moura, Ellen Reynolds, Corinna Richards, Julie Richardson, Thomas Richardson, Charlotte Riche, Angela Maxine Risner, Helen Roberts, Genevieve Robinson, James Roditi, Paul Roebuck, Aurelia Rogalli, Oliver Rogers, Lauren Rooney, Alan Rose, Philippa Ross, Peter Rostron, Ilaria Rovera, Christopher Rowland, Dave Rowlands, Emile Ruddock, Ro Ruiz-Ochoa, Nick Rundall, Adrienne Russell, Megan Russell, Emma Ryan, Richard Sackey-Addo, Emily Sadler, Miranda Salter, Danielle Sampson, Prad Samtani, Eduardo Sanchez-Seco, Zé Sandell, Julee Sanderson, Grishma Santosh, Ivan Sanz, Dominique Sapsin, Claire Sargent, Jasminder Kaur Satnam Singh, Anya Sayadian, Katherine

Sayce, Charlotte Scott, Elliott Scott, Helen Scott, Lewis Searle, Oliver Sears, Kathrin Selbmann, Jenny Selden, Amy Sell, Lee Selvarajah, Viki Sena, Carole Shackleton, Baldip Shah, Melinda Shalet, Priya Shah, Rahim Shamji, Kimberley Shamtally, Radhika Shanmuganathan, Sara Shao, Jyoti Sharma, Kitty Sheppard, Matthew Sherr, Amit Sheth, Jacqueline Shirley, Chris Shoubridge, Alessandra Shurina, Nishtah Sian, Siphosenkosi Sibindi, Emilie Silkoset, Kimbo Silver, Natasha Simpson, Grainne Sinclair, Munjeet Singh, Katherine Sivieng, Hayley Smith, Caroline Smith, Cedric Smith, David Smith, David Smith, Eve Smith, Hannah Smith, Janesia Smith, Janine Smith, Joanna Smith, Kay Smith, Pippa Smith, Susan Smith, James Smy, Barry Smyth, Marc Snell, Bhavesh Solanki, Daria Solovyeva, Yuchen Song, Olly Soper, Deidre Sorensen, Robert Sparrow, Todd Speakman, Ezra Spearpoint, Dan Spence, Matt Squires, Vaishnavee Sreeharan, Mark Stanborough, Ashley Leanne Steed, Chloe Stephens, Katie Stephenson, Paul Stevens, Ted Stevens, Amanda Stewart, Andy Stillwell, Andrew Stimson, Emma Stoffer, Rhona Elva Stokes, Emma Stone, Peter Stone, Peter Stoyanov, Elena Sukhova, Lilith Sumesar-Rai, Jack Summerfield, Roberto Surace, Simon Surtees, Carole Anne Sutcliffe, Chris Sutton, Tommy Swale, Kate Swallow, Dan Swann, Rebecca Sweeney, Hayley Syme, Taj Taak, Toyomi Takeda, Aaron Tanice, Elba Tapia Montes, Martin Tatem, Jessica Tatnell, Joanne Tay, Alastair Taylor, Dougal Taylor, Julie Taylor, Siobhan Taylor, Victoria Taylor, Adele Teague, Leslie Thelwall, Oliver Thelwall, Della Thielamay, Robert Thomas, Abraham Thomas, Sophie Thomas, Steve Thompson, Mary Thorogood, Joanne Thorpe, Cat Thrower, Eleanor Thrower, Justine Thrower, Helena Tidey, Wayne Tieken, Mark Tierney, Aileen Toal, Areta Toalima, Anna Tomlinson, Frances Touch, Gary Tough, Liam Tracey, Shyvonne Trench, Joanne Trim, Giulio Troccoli, Patricia Trott, Paul Trumble, Clare Tsangari, Bonny Turner, Clare Turner, Lorna Turner, Sam Turner, Shreena Turner, Agatha Uchendu, Calum Upton, Umut Uysal, Preeti Vadgama, Sree Vallipuram Vallipuram, Jess Veale, Jan-Vincent Velazco, Andrew Verney, Laura Viander, Rosemary Vidad, Ella Virr, Katie Vorontsova, David Walach, Wendy Walach, Adam Walsh, Peter Walsh, David Walter, Wenjing Wang, Shukai Wang, Emily Ward, Victoria Ward, Roy Wareham, Ewan Watson, John Watkins, Ray Watters, Richard Watts, Christopher Welch, Amber Wells, Andrew Wells, Susannah Wells, Emma West, Dan Weymouth, Christopher Whalen, Stuart Whatmore, Kate Whitaker, Aimee White, Ruth White, Nyome Whitfield, Jonny Whitmore, Chris Whyley, Gemma Whyley, Keith Wickham, Amy Wicks, Lettice Wigby, Peter Wildman, Laura Wiles, Linda Wilkinson, Anthony Williams, Bethan Williams, Cat Williams, Deren Williams, Jane Williams, Jonathan Williams, Samantha Jane C Williams, Tracey Williams, Tahirah Williams Espinosa, Georgette Wills, Dave Wilson, Jane Wilson, Phi Wilson, Emma Winchester, Ellie Wingett, Jim Wingfield, Avenell Winston, Henry Wood, Jeremy Wood, Katey Wood, Natasha Wood, David Woods, Peter Wooldridge, Steve Woolmore, Mark Wootton, Michael Worthington, Dave Wright, Gillian Wright, Louise Wright, Bian Wu, Luke Wyeth, Zhiqiang Xiao, Taylor Xu, Jing Yang, Xiaoqian Yang, Rukhsana Yaqoob, Iris Yau, Wai-Lun Yip, Nava Yoganathan, Elaine Young, Vera Yu, Omolara Yusuff, Aliki Zachariadi, Aivars Zarins, Violeta Zepinic, Chen Zhang, Chen Zhang, Lisa Zhang, Qingshan Zhang, Qinhan Zhang, Xinran Zhang, Yunqian Zhang, Jia Zhao, Lucy Zidour Mcstravick **Here Comes the Sun** Emma Adams, Ayoola Alase, Nuno Almeida, Lauren Azania Aymer-Jeffrey, Alice Bailey-Kennedy, Jess Bale, Gup Bansal, Jennifer Barker, Sarah Barson, Helen Batch, Kim Bell, Nathan Benson, Kelly Bentley, Laura Bilous, Fay Birch, Naomi Blowes, Emma Bolton, Natasha Boyle, Thomas Brackley, Lucy Brennan, Megan Brock, Laura Brown, Lizzy Brown, Monique Brown, Andrew Burnett, Grace Byrne, Sorcha Byrne, Lucy Calvert, Jo Chapman, Kirsty Cherrett, Yvette Claireaux, Peter Clerkin, Emily Cobie, Nicoletta Constantinou, Justin Creasey, Matthew Cressey, Corrinne Curtis, Ellie Curtis, Ryan Curtis, Victoria Davis, Fran Dearlove, Carmen Dennis, Dmitry Devetyarov, Audrey Doklan, Hannah Dolan Davies, Stacey Dorling, Renee Dowuona-Ocran, Charlotte Dutton, Samantha Edgcombe, Mischa Evans-Giraud, Abigail Everett, Amy Ferguson, Ella Fleetwood, Kate Foster, Kelly-Ann Fry, Esther Fuge, Sammy Furnival, Adesuwa Gbinigie, Amy Goodman, Carly Grant, Lucy Gratton, Charelle Griffith, Gemma Griffiths, Katrina Guibarra, Mitchell Hadley, Lottie Hall, Carmen Harris, Kayley Harrison, Theresa Heinen, Jessica Hemingway, Katie Herbert, Isabelle Hetherington, Sophie Hirst, Charlotte Hunter, Shakira Hylton, Gabi Ivorra-Morell, Hina Jansari, Katy Jasper, Asha Jennings-Grant, Danielle Jones, Lauren Lee Jones, Imogen Joyce, Rachel Keenan, Carrie-Louise Knight, Irene Konsolou, Callum Kumar-Shaw, Kirsty Lack, Pui Yee Lai, Victoria Lamm, Adelaide Lane, Luke Lawar, Sammie Jo Leicester, Jayred Lempriere, Tom Leonard, Jeremy Lilley, Sophie Lowen, Jenni Lynch, Hannah Madden, Alexandra Mann, Kate Manning, Ceri Jayne Marin, Alex Marsh, Tanyel Mayin, Emily Mcallister Brown, Yasmin Mccullough, Steph Mcmillan, Engin Mehmet, Charlotte Milligan, Michael Mogridge, Veronica Monk, Holly Moore, Mell Mroch, Louise Mulcrone, Sophie Musson, Sian Myers, Aliye Nafi, Nikoletta Nicolaou, Debbie Nielsen, Rebecca Page, Tys Panayis, Chun Ling Pang, Harriet Parker-Beldeau, Helen Parsons, Alicia Pattyson, Sophie Paulson, Sherry Platts, Nikki Pocklington, Ben Pomeroy, Patrick Porto, Kerry Powell, Lindsey Pryor, Bethany Pyner, Philip Quigley, Jennifer Reynolds, Ellen Rowley, Rackelle Rutherford, Emily Rutherwood, Holly Sands, Victoria Schaverien, Giulia Settomini, Natalie Shall, Rosie Shaw, Jen Shutter, Lauren Siddall, Bianca Silcox, Juliane Silveira, Fiona Skidmore, Catherine St Bean, Georgie St. Juste, Katie Stapleton, Emma Sterling, Fallon Stocker, Mai Tassinari, Kirstie Taylor, Ella Thiele, Tanya Tominey, Sarah Tomlinson, Esther Tuakli, Lily Turner, Wendy Tweedle, Rachel Twinn, Holly Unnuk, Rosie Unwin, James Wakeling, Tara Walker, Caldy Walton, Hollie Ware, Stephanie Warwick, Jemma Patricia Watling, Vaughan Watts, Sarah Webber, Nathan Wharton, Louise Wheeler, Nicola Whetton, Hannah White, Bethany Whiteley, Sally Wignall, Wanida Woharn, Bileigh Wood, Katy Woodley, Lindsay Woodman, Megan Wooldridge, Emma Woolston, Josephine Worsop, Corina Wuersch, Lucy Yang **A Symphony of British Music** James Ackroyd, Sally Adams, Sophie Adams, Mary Agbro, Judith Agnew, Jaspal Aiden, Bernie Aitken, Bola Ajayi, Bolu Akindoyin, Fallon Alexis, Daniel Aley, Ben Allcock, Georgia Allright, Andrew Almond, Clare Almond, Alexandra Amargianitakis, Pippa Andre, Alex Antoniou, Naima Anwar, Anthony Appleton, Zoe Armfield, Alessandro Ascani, Sally Ashton, Sarah Ashton, Justin Ashworth, Ama Asiedu, Scott Atkins, Simon Aukland, Helen Theofanous Avery, Mahmoud Azzam, Aaron Bailey, Alex Bailey-Dumetz, Alex Bajcar, Ricky Bakanowski, Sundeep Singh Bangar, Karen Banner, Helen Barker, Suzanna Barnes, Adam Barriball, Sanjeet Bedi, Damian Bell, Harry Bell, Megan Bennett, Mike Benson, Diana Bereczki, Alfredo Bernaez, Lizelle Bester, Gowinder Bhambhra, Pranav Bhanot, Jonathan Billins, Charlotte Bilsby, Charlotte Binney, David Birch, Sandy Birk, Naomi Bishop, Jack Bishop, Katie Black, Yolanda Blades, Laura Blake, Lane Blanchard, Eva Blanco, Phillip Bodenham, Jeremy Booth, Jonathan Booth, Tom Bowen, Sherilyn Boyd, James Boyle, Julie Brame, Molly Brame, Diane Bramley, Selina Ursula Brathwaite, Anna Breheny, Katherine Brent, Neil Brent, Ellen Brereton, Bella Broad, Stephanie Brown, Warren James Brown, Daniel Brownridge, Kerrine Bryan, Stuart Bumford, Paul Bunford, Francesca Burgess, Patrick Burke, Rachel Burn, Lynne Burnham, Greg Butler, Samuel Butler, Elisa Buttle, Vicki Bye, Giorgio Cacioppo, Justin Caesar, Hannah Cameron, Stuart Cameron, Aimee Campbell, Chloe Campbell, Kelsey Campbell, Lucien Campbell, Sarah Campbell, Tanya Campbell, Victoria Campbell, Hayley Capp, Elise Carman, Chrissie Carpenter, Emily Carpenter, Quin Casey, Rebekah Castle, Liam Caulfield, Anjalee Chakravarty-Agbo, Geoffrey Chang King, David Chaplin, Matthew Chaplin, Richard Chapman, Rebecca Charlton, Ramneek Chawla, Kay Child, Barry Cho, Stacey Chouvier-Taylor, Kirsten Clay, Christian Clemares Sibils, Lottie Clitherow, Andrew Close, Faye Clough, Graham Gallacher Cochran, Richard Coffey, Tristan Cogswell, Jim Collier, Elena Collins, Sophie Constantine, Michael Conway, Eleanor Cooke, Rachel Cooke, Bill Copland, Lesley Copland, Jamie Corner, Alexandra Cornwell, Shanice Corr, Erica Cortopassi, Karen Coulthard, Susanna Cousins, Ashleigh Cox, Hazel Crabb-Wyke, Edward Crann, James Craven, Trisha Cray, Louise Croft, Daisy Croker, David Crosby, Laura Crosby, Javi Cucarella-Carretero, Carmela Curatolo, Millie Curd, David Curran, Alexia D'Amato, Yasmin Dan, Molly Darracott, Lydia Davidson, Annita Davies, Emma-Jayne Davies, Mabeth Davies, Michael Davies, Paul Davies, Scout Davies, Steve Davies, Jerry Lee Dawson, Kate-Lily De Graft-Johnson, Cristine De Paula, Christopher Dech, Harkirat Singh Degun, Joanna Dent, Barbara Denyer, Satinder Dhadda, Rajnandan Dhariwal, Simer Kaur Dhaliwal, Ciara Diamond, Louise Dinnage, Nicky Donald, Peri-Jay Donovan, Camilla Dowling, Andrew Downing, David Downing, Jaspreet Duhra, Laurence Dunford, Eva Dunn, Catherine Durkin, Paul Edkins, Hannah Edwards, Maria Egwea-Seleznova, David Ellis, Michael Ellis, Eve Elwell, Donal Emerson, Simon Emery, Lola Eniraiyetan, Richelle Eriksson, Alex Evans, Lucy Evans, Lauren Evans, Nicole Eve, Stephen Everett, Armelle Everingham, Hady Ezzeldin, Olivia Fairclough, Daniel Fairhall, Jeffrey Fairman, Simon Fairman, Valentine Falchero, Nikki Feld, David Ferguson, Timothy Field, Sarah Fildes, David Finlayson, Jemma Fisher, Persephone Fitzpatrick, Sorrel Fitzpatrick, Elaine Fleming, Elizabeth Fleming, Heather Fleming, Elaine Foley, Marie Forbes, André Francis, Jennifer Francis, Tenniel Francis, Lydia Fraser-Ward, Aaron Frazer, Gem Freeman, Sarah Freeman, Oliver Freer-Ash, Suraj Gadar, Sushil Gadar, Amaya Gallego, Lauren Garbutt, Peter Garden, Martin Garnett, Aleena George, Pammy Georgieva, Rajni Ghir, Samantha Gibbons, Emily Gibbs, Ian Gibbs, Benedict Gibson, Rosalind Gibson, Joel Gilbert, Michael Gilbert, Pauline Gill, Susie Gill, Emma Goldhawk, April Goodall, Sophie Goodwin, Fiona Gordon, Clare Gore, George Gorzynski, Mark Gostick, Karina Gould, Rachel Graham, Agris Graveris, Maria Gray, Stacey Gray, Hannah Greaves, Annie Green, Fiona Green, Jonathan Green, Rachel Greene, Eleanor Greene, Lamisha Green-Roberts, Victoria Greenway, Jessica Greer, Alistair Groves, Lee Grubb, Sirjana Gurung, Helga Gutmane, Joanna Gwynne, Das Halaith, Bradley Hall, Tim Hall, Keith Hallam, Natalie Hall-Swan, Rob Halpin, Claire Hamer, Rebecca Hammond, Munet Hara, Jessamy Hardie, Bethany Harris, Janice Hart, Anya Harvey, Vikta Harvey, David Haskins, Grace Hately, Kirstie Hawkes, Paul Hawkridge, Elize Haygarth-Farrer, Fran Hayward, Francesca Head, Amy Heap, Anthony Hearn, Kate Hearn, John Hedges, Catherine Hegarty, Anna Hejnar, Thora Helgadottir, Katy Helps, Joanna Hemming, Lauren Henry, Jo Hensman, Emma Heraghty , Ellie Herold, Amy Higgins, Rosanna High, Hastings Hill, Lucy Hillier, George Hixson, Nicola Hoile, Gary Holden, Lara Holford, Iona Holland, Claire Holman, Rob Honeywood, Chantelle Hooley, Richard Hopkin, Geraint Hopkins, Tom Horswell, Angela Housden, Lynda How, Mark Howe, Louise Howells, Hollie Hubbard, Victoria Huggins, Anthony Hughes, Kevin Hughes, Steve Hughes, David Hurlbut, Jessica Hyde, Sarah Impey, Dru Impleton, Richelle Isaacs, Matthew Isherwood, Maureen Isherwood, Kate Izzard, Adrian Jackson, Philip Jakeman, Adrian James, John Jamieson, Baljinder Kaur Jassi, Lionel Jeffery, Dan Jenkins, Kiranjeet Jhangaria, Lee Johnson, Hannah Johnson, Stephanie Johnson, Gethin Jones, Margaret Jones, Michael Jones, Rachel Jones, Robert Jones, Hayley Jordan, Sumeet Singh Josh, Veda Joslin, Adam Joyce, Robert Jukes, Karan Singh Kalsi, Siu Mun Kam, Robin Kamath, Kaypreet Kandola, Asiya Kapysheva, Danielle Kassarate, Garminder Kaur, Melinda Kaur, Alex Kay, Sarah Kearley, Bernadine Kearns, Sean Jamie Keating , Lois Keeton, Hilarie Kerr, Georgie Keyes, Taz Khan, Lloyd Kilford, Alan King, Anna King, Claire King, Isi King, Lauren King, Nicola King, Orla King, Simon King, Tom King, Chris Kinsman, Margaret Kirby, Helena Knight, Russell Knight, Tomomi Kosano, Maxim Kotenev, Timea Kovacs, Kerttu Kulasepp, Sylvia Lahav, Mavis Lai, Anna Langford, Bharat Lard, Juliet Lashbrook, Antonelio Lasic, Dave Latcham, Peter Laurie, David Lawley, Sarah Lawrence, Stephanie Lawrence, Alys Leach, Tim Leadbetter, Dale Lee, Kate Lennon, Gundhild Lenz-Mulligan, Louise Levene, Eirian Lewis, Gareth Lewis, Geraint Lewis, Aurelie L'Hostis, Ben Lightfoot, Steve Lillistone, Becky Ling, Javier Llanos, Doug Lloyd Haynes, Hannah Lockyer, Anthony Loddo, Claire Long, John Long, Verity Long, Judith Lorde, Lia Loukas, Dimitra Louskas, Catherine Loveless, Oleksii Lytvynov, Harriet Maas, John Macdonald, George Macpherson, Monika Madej, Saloni Madhok, Petrus Madutlela, Harry Magnall, Lindsey Major, Colin Malam, Georgina Mandefield, Kulbinder Mann, Theresa Manns, Brian Mansfield, Wajahat Mansoor, Laura Marshall, Paul Martin, Robert Martin, Romain Martin, Inderjeet Marwhay , Tj Mason, Kirandip Kaur Matharu, Wendy Mathews, Gill Matson, Boyd Matthews, Stergios Mavrikis, Oliver Mayo, Gordon McAnespie, Olivia Mcaulay, Diego Mccarthy, Stephanie Mcclellan, Tom Mccormack, Ellie McGowan, Steve Mcgrath, Fliss Mcgreal, Mark Mckenzie-Ray, Katharine Mcnamara, Terrie-May Mcnulty, Laura McQuaid, Abi Mctear, Carel Meganck, Alex Meredith, Rob Meredith, James Merrell, John Meyers, Paul Middleton, Brian Millar, Louise Minter, Polina Mladenova, Melissa Mok, Rebecca Monnington, Tori Moone, Maureen Mordi, Lucy Morgan, Kirsten Morgan, Lee Moriarty, Bethan Morris, Steve Morris, Anthony Mortimer, Gemma Morton, Hayley Morton, Andrew Moss, Olivia Moss, Rory Mudie, Anne Muir, Jenni Mullane, Josie Mullen, Jim Mulligan, Jesus Munoz, Tom Murchu, Laura Murphy, Olivia Murphy, Rebecca Murphy, Teresa Murray, Rachel Mylon, Ravi Nagra, Claire Neate, Andrew Needham, Bethany Nelson, Myles Newland, Graham Newson, Chinwe Nnajiuba, Ruth Noble, Felicity Noonan, Graham Norman, Tabitha Norman-Clarke, Erin Norris, Jennifer Norris, Nodge Norris, Marcelino Noya-Rey, Karin Nyqvist, Charlotte O' Connell, Jodie Oakes, Layo Obembe, Rebecca O'Brien, Pawel Obrocki, Evelyn Ofori-Kuragu, Eniye Ogieva, Ciara O'Heneghan-Yates, Kingsley Okoli, Jojo Oldham, Pete Oldroyd, Abi Oliver, Fid Oppong Bassuah, Emily Orme, Carly-Joy Osborne, Claire Osborne, Toby Osborne, Karen Osman, Pete Osman, Rodphi Pandinuela, Tejinder Singh Panesar, Ricki Paraskevas, Amy Parker, Neil Parker, Paul Parsonage, Natalie Parsons, Ricky Patel, Ron Paterson, Michailia Patterson, Rachel Patterson, Holly Penalver, Nic Perandin, Daniel Perez Krause, Joe Pharoah, Joseph Phillips, Rossana Piazzini, Rafal Pilinski, Craig Pitman, Harry Planche, Lizzy Playford, Caroline Pooley, Stephanie Potter, Cassius Powell, Kate Pritchard, Amy Probert, Lucy Pryor, Jhovany Puerta Palacio, Masha Punchak, Jattinder Purewal, Sian Quinn, Antony Rabin, Tee Raheem, Prem Rai, Sabie Rainton, Sumira Raja, Zoe Randle, Natasha Ratcliffe, Gurpreet Singh Rattan, Sam Rawlings, Kirsty Rayfield, Manminder Rayit, Max Raymond, Samantha Rayner, Joanna Reber, Kelly Reeve, Valentina Regoli, Gurdeep Rehinsi, Gurbind Singh Rehinsi, Maiga Reinharde, Sameratu Rettew, Max Reynolds, Roderick Rhys-Jones, Jessica Richards, Emma Richardson, Lauren Riley, Peter William Michael Ritch, Kathryn Robb, Graham Roberts, Huw Roberts, Robert Roberts, Florence Roberts-Bowman, Andrew Robinson, Rosanna Robinson, Tina Robinson , Geovanny Rocha Hernandez, Carlos Roche, Geoff Rogers, Jessica Rogers, Stephen Ronan, Cecilia Rosales, Eleanor Rossiter, Philippa Rossiter, Peter Rowlstone, Amanda Royes, Lucy Ruglen, Natasha Rukazenkova, Jasdeep Rupra, Alice Russell, Tom Russell, Val Russell, Ben Rutt-Howard, Clare Rydon, Lewis Rylands, Gemma Salm, Tej Samra, Rhydian Sandbrook, Amraaj Sandhu, Karampreet Sandhu, Manraj Sandhu, Matthew Sandiford, Lakhbir Singh Sangha, Sukhbir Singh Sangha, Sunbir Singh Sangha, Will Scarnell, Simone Schmidt, Julia Schneider, Friesia Schuil, Mario Scinto, Clare Scott, Colleen Scott, Rosie Secker, Harpreet Sekhon, Indunee Seneviratne, Shreena Shah, Kokil Sharma, David Sharpe, Dieter Shaw, Christine Shead, Lucy Shitova, Mary Sibley, Charles Sim , Sharone Simpson, Olly Simpson, Tirath Singh, Gavin Skinner, Mick Skrzypiec, Cath Slade, Jon Slater, Jonathan Slaughter, Charlotte Smith, Daisy Smith, David Smith, Freya Smith, Peter Smith, Rebecca Smith, Laura Smith O'Driscoll, Grace Smithen, Joss Smithson, Esther Smyth, Richard Snowdon, Raj Sohpal, Parabjeet Souni, Danielle Spears, Gareth Streeter , Hannah Suthren, Dave Sweet, Rachael Sykes, Rob Sykes, James Tait, Jayne Tarbuck, Colin Taylor, John Taylor, Katherine Taylor, Jo Taylor-Medhurst, Kheng Teh, Lynda Thomas, Pamela Thompson, Tommo Thomson, John Thornely, Stephanie Thorpe, Christopher Tipler, Stephanie Tipping, Lexie Titterington, Alice Triffitt, Klaudia Trzcielinska, Charlotte Tuffen, Nadine Turk, Sandra Turkiewicz, Stephen Turner, Curzon Tussaud, Harry Tweddell, Claire Tweedie, Lauren Tyas, Helena Varley, Alan Vaughan, Juan Veloza Vargas, Victoria Vickers, Richard Vigars, Harkiran Virdee, Victoria Wägner, Hannah Wainwright, Kathryn Wakefield, Katie Walker, Leanne Walker, Philip Walter, Keith Warren, Kathryn Warrilow, Ruth Waters, Martin Watts, Abigail Watts-Cherry, Carol Weatherley, Caroline Webb, Cher Webb, Kate Weston, Olivia Whalley, Natalie Wheaton, Phillip Whittenham, Owen Wick, Aaron Wilkins, Geoffrey Williams, Mark Williams-Jones, Carolyn Williamson, Claire Wilson, Xanthe Wilson, Hannah Wing, Siobhan Witter, Shirley Wood, Steven Wood, Kim Woodward, Sarah Woodward, Georgina Wootten, Gareth Worth, Emily Wright, Lucy-Linda Wright, Fleur Wylie, James Yan, Cherry Yeandle, Hannah Yeoman, Emily Yoon, Vivienne Youell, Sondes Youssef, David Znak **Closing of the Games** Laurence Adams, Peter Barnes, Nicholas Brown, Cameron Carr, Arthur Charlesworth, Colin Davies, Derek Davies, Nigel Davis, Graeme Dawson, Edward Edwards, Ian Edwards, John Edwards, Berwyn Evans, Peter Gasson, Paul Gordon, Malcolm Harkett, Barry Howard, Brian Johnson, Colin Jones, Richard Jones, David Keep, Erik Kerr, Simon Laight, Donald

Volunteers
Bénévoles

May, James Milanovic, David Morgan, John O'Brien, Philip Olsen, Richard Owen, Michael Perry, Mark Robson, John Shackleford, Philip Stewart, Alwyn Thomas, Neil Thorneycroft, Tom Underhill, Thomas Wilcox Jones, John Williams, Nigel Williams, Francis Wilson, Thomas Windsor **Spirit of the Flame** Nadia Abdulla, Rhianwen Adam, Jade Adams, Kei Akahoshi, Demi Aldred, Hayley Allen, Hannah Allsop, Kerry-Anne Ashcroft, Emily Ayers, Hannah Badge, Desiree Ballantyne-Grove, Sophie Baxter, Reena Bhattacharjee, Stephanie Bikow, Kerry Birkett, Georgina Blackwell, Sara Jane Bloor, Grace Blundell, Lauren Borthwick, Mica Bradbury, Naomi Brehm, Bethany Bresnen, Rosie Bretherton, Lucy Burns, Anna Burrows, Ellie Byrne, Kate Byrne, Fiona Cameron Martin, Niki Campbell, Maria Begona Cao Miranda, Alice Carden, Nicola Carroll, Eva Chambers, Emma Collingwood, Jacqueline Coombs, Natasha Cox, Shannon Craik Rpd, Lauren Crispin, Dominique Densmore, Alexandra Desvignes, Olivia Devyea, Louise Dobing, Sachiko Doi, Jo Dooher, Hannah Douglas, Madeleine Dowdney, Chloe Dowell, Milly Doyle, Andria Drousiotou, Charlotte Dunn, Samantha Dyer, Sarah Ellisdon, Emily Evans, Jess Evans, Hannah Faid, Vanessa Fenton, Victoria Ferguson, Laurretta Ferrari Summerscales, Kiri Fitzgerald, Lavinia Fitzpatrick, Nikisha Fogo, Eleanor Forrest, Laura Forsyth, Nefeli Fotiadi, Emily Francis, Elanore Franklin, Olivia Gaston, Emma Gatt, Raquel Gaviria, Chiara Gibbs, Katie Gibson, Eve Gilliland, Lillia Gilliland, Hazel Gold, Sophie Greenstreet, Maria Grisafi, Marija Grozova, Natalie Jayne Hall, Sophie Hall, Tiffany Hamilton-Atkins, Laura Hammond, Jennifer Harrington, Zoe Harrower, Alexandra Hart, Ashley Harvey, Emma Hatton, Clare Haven, Lucinda Hennessy, Nicola Henshall, Lorea Hernández Marquinez, Lotte Hill, Megan Hill, Emily Hook, Grace Horler, Emily Horner, Eloise Horton, Atsuko Hotate, Lily Howes, Emily Hughes-Lewis, Amber Hunt, Anna Marie Idle, Sita Jobanputra, Jennifer Jones, Stephanie Jones, Malika Jones, Katie Kelly, Emily Kerr, Holly Kirkwood, May Kwok, Perdita Jayne Lancaster, Vicky Lardner, Phoebe Latham Wake, Abi Lawman, Elodie Lawrence, Jenna Lee, Olivia Leek, Cíara Lightholder, Kate Lindley, Alexandra Lowe, Sophie Malpass, Carrie Marsden, Sarah-Jane Maunder, Lara Mccabe, Ashling Mccann, Lucy Mcferran, Fiona McGee, Ashleigh Mcilhone, Victoria Mcnaughton, Gemma Melhuish, Olivia Mellodey, Helena Micklethwaite, Frankie Morris, Laura Morse, Abigail Murray, Rosanna Nevard, Cassie Newby, Lucy Newman, Monica Nicolaides, Dani Nieuwenhuys, Charlotte Nolan, Hannah Northern, Erin O' Toole, Charlotte O'Brien, Monja Obrul, Sarah O'Connell, Nicole O'Neill, Suzan Opperman, Ksenia Ovsyanick, Laura Palmer, Rachel Parker, Kimberley Pena, Francesca Peplow, Lucia Piquero Alvarez, Danielle Plummer, Chantelle Poole, Natalie Potter, Natalia Potter Wood, Kayla Poulton, Louise Powell, Sarah Pritchard, Lisa Probert, Stina Quagebeur, Caroline Rees, Charlotte Ring, Laura Robinson, Kate Roe-Brown, Verena Roth, Chantel Roulston, Nikita Ruhl, Valentina Russo, Jacqueline Ryan, Nadia Sadiq, Michelle Samson, Katie Saunders, Samantha Ceyda Saygilier, Hannah Seamons, Rebecca Sewell, Eleanor Sharpe, Grace Simmons, Izzy Sleeman, Charlotte-Emma Soffe, Jade Spooner, Tamarin Stott, Lynsey Sutherland, Hannah Thomas, Kelly Thomson, Joanne Thwaite, Sophie Tickle, Sayako Tomiyoshi, Diem Tran Thi Ngoc, Maud Helene Treille, Claire Tyler, Rachel Urquhart, Alexandra Varese, Laura Vercoe, Ella Walker, Ellie Warner, Jessie Waterfield, Kate Webster, Rosie Williams, Olivia Willoughby, Jordan Wing, Kit Sum Wong, Alicia Woodhouse, Araminta Wraith, Georgia Yiannakas, Anthi Ziliki **Creative Team** Makayla Abraham, Ash Sohyun Ahn, Caroline Akselson, Jessica Albon, Tanya Alexander, Fatima Ali, Nazia Ali, Jahir Ali, Louise Allberry, Jennifer Allen, Justin Allin, Josephine Allitt, Shaimaa Alruwaished, Hana Amer, Katherine Anderson, Ashley Andrews, Maria Anning, Alicia Apaloo-Edwards, Jack Appleyard, Helene Arnesen, Isabella Asimadi, Storm Athill, Sophia Austen-Meek, Sian Ayres, Yvonne Bailey, Mathura Balanadarasan, Sophie Bann, Claire Bannister, Rebecca Barclay, Penelope Bardoni, Lyndsey Barnewell, Matej Barszcz, Tonia Bastyan, Dean Batte, Natalie Beales, Daisy Beattie, Anna Beckett, Apia Begum, Shahania Begum, Shamama Begum, Katie Bell, Eki Belo-Osagie, Carol Belston, Charlotte Bentham, Piotr Berkowicz, Agathe Bernardon, Deepti Bhalla, Sobia Bhatti, Grant Bigland, Jennifer Bigland, Gemma Bishop, Poppy Biswell, Chloe Blake, Matthew Blount, Kathleen Boland, Anna Bonomi, Natasha Bott, Charlotte Boulton, E Boussekson, Katie-May Boyd, Eve Bradshaw, Geno Brantley, Molly Bray, Eve Brayshaw, Bernadette Brennan, Eleanor Brereton, Amy Brian, Ross Britten, Charlotte Brook, Gregory Brown, Claire Bunyard, Tazmin Burr, Lily Burrows, Eleanor Butcher, Lauren Butler, Sarah-Jane Caddock, Luman Cai, Fabianne Calitri, Grace Cameron, Charlotte Campbell, Stuart Campbell, Lisa Carracedo, Rachel Carter, Danielle Casey, Bridget Cass, Amy Cassell, Ella Chadwick, Bonnie Chai, Kit Shuen Chan, Yu Hui Chan, Ying Tung Chan, Rosie Chaplin, Nadine Chapman, Jason Charles, Grace Cheetham, Szu-Jung Chen, Viviane Chen, Eponone Chen, Dong Hoon Choi, Joanna Christou, Lidia Cimule, Loren Clark, Emma Connor, Victoria Conte, Alison Convery, Adam Cookson, Eleanor Coole-Green, Anne Cooper, Shaun Corcoran, Helga Cory-Wright, Florence Court, Chloe Cowan, Zac Coyle, Alex Crawford, Alexandra Cresswell, Amy Cresswell, Emma Cresswell, Connie Croasdale, Mary Cuffe, Mary Cuffe, Danielle Cullen, Henrietta Curtis, Anna Czerniavska, David Daglish, Miriam Damanhuri, Alice Dan, Sharna David, Gabrielle Davies, Frances Davies, Holly Davies, Lucy Davis, Julia Day, Amy De Rees, Daniel Defreitas, Amy DeRees, Amanda Derrick, Joana Dias, Claire Docherty, Rebecca Doidge, Tatiana Dolmatovskaya, Blake Douglas, Harriet Dyson, Danielle Eagles, Anthony Earles, Harriette Earp, Samantha Easey, Joanna East, Carolyn Ebanks, Katie Eden, Georgina Edwards, Bryony Edwards, Maja Ehliar, Charlotte England, Gemma Evans, Constantina Evriviadou, Tobias Fairclough, Josie Falconer, Aileen Faller, Jonathan Fensom, Sophie Finch, Wendy Foggin, Charley Fone, Edwin Ford, Rebecca Forknall, Luca Formica, Jessica Fournier D'Albe, Samantha Fox, Melissa Francis, Christabel Franklin, Chloe French, Marjorie Frick, Gemma Friel, Momoko Fujiwara, Katie Garden, Ruby Gaskell, Suchen Ge, Lauren Gee, Noella Geoghegan, Eleanor Gibson, Enka Gill, Caroline Gladwin, Beata Goaszweska, Joanna Goodman, Danielle Grant, Elizabeth Grant, Jessica Green, Elaine Guillon, Tharanga Gunawardena, Karen Gurney, Sandra Gustafsson, Zlatka Halkova, Melissa Hall, Jessica Halsey, Holly Hamblin, Kim Hamilton, Meng Hao, Alissa Harger, Iyo Hasegawa, Geraldine Hawkins, Alison Haworth, Jemma Haywood, Florence Hazard, Celestine Healy, Emma Heard, Audrey Elizabeth Hedgecock, Chloe Henderson, Holly Rose Henshaw, Clare Hepburn, Abigail Hernon, Francesca Hey, Amy Hickie, George Hims, Lysette Hodgson, Ruby Hodgson, Alix Holdaway-Salmon, Scarlett Hooper, Rachel Hopper, Sarah Hosein, Tina Hsu, Shuyi Huang, Chanel Huang, Jessica Hughes, Rosina Humphrey, Joanna Hunnisett, Toria Hunt, Jamila Hussain, Michelle Huynh, Silje Isaksen, Nur Ismail, Annan Jaggernauth, Gillian Jarvis, Rebecca Jempson, Madeleine Jenkins, Laura Jenkins, Katie Jenkinson, Laura Jenkinson, Charlotte Jepson, Amy Job, Bob Johnson, Margaret Johnson, Natasha Johnson, Georgia Jones, Lucy Jones, Rebecca Jones, Sophia Joseph, Eleanor Joyce, Holly Judd, Elizabeth Kane, Abul Kasam, Abul Kasam, Megan Keegan, Holly Keen, Tanya Keen, Muireann Kelly, Charlotte Kelly, Kristine Kenmochi, Ahhyun Kim, Joseph Kim-Suzuki, Harriet Kings, Leanne Kinnie, Osnat Koblenz, Veronika Kovacikova, Igli Kroqi, Georgina Lamb, Darren Lancett, Alexandra Langman, Sophie Langsford, Sara Laratro, Josie Lee, Tom Leggat, Demelza Leng, Caroline Lewis, Ge LI, Yangyang Li, Ruoxuan Li, Shuang Liang, Kate Lithgow, Roberta Lockett, Narash Lohia, Sue Lowe, Antonia Lynch, Emilie Lyons, Amy Macpherson, Emma Madray, Sara Maggi, Beverley Magtibay, Saad Mahmood, Rebecca Mahoney, Maria Mantilla, Ivan Manzella, Kathryn Marooney, Joanna Marshall, Freya Martin, Sierra Martin, Anna Martin, Tasha Marvell, John May, Ann-Marie Mays, Tansy McCluskie, Pete McDonagh, Jo McDonald, Sammi McGuigan, Michelle McHale, Letitia McLaughlin, Dorothy McLennan, Amy McPherson, Laura Meichtry, Olivia Catherine Mellowes, Cheramour Meoquanne, Florence Meredith, Gabrielle Milanese, Stephanie Miles, Jennifer Millen, Darci Miller, Dan Miller, Bo-Kyung Min, Clodagh Miskelly, Jasumati Mistry, Hannah Mitchell, Connor Mitchell, Sabrina Mohamed, Abigail Moller, Paula Gonzalez Montecino, Rosey Morling, Ronan Morrow, Madalaine Mould, Jillian Murray, Yuki Nakamura, Kamal Natt, Chloe Newman, Candice Newton, Billy Yu Lok Ng, Mandy Ngo, Fern Nolan, Jo Noon, Tanya Noor, Biannca Nugent, Michael Offei, Tosin Ogunsanya, Rebecca O'Higgins, Christina Omideyi, Zanna Orage, Zeanab Oshinbolu, Rainelle Osuji, Priscilla Otema, Lucy Packham-O'Brien, Sharon Page, Georgia Paget, Samuella Palmer, Natasha Payne, Donna Pendarvis, J. Childe Pendergast, Manavi Perera, Cathy Perkins, Fong Perry, Shamaela Perwiz, Louise Phelan, Gloria Enechojo Philip, Sabina Piccini, Hannah Pick, Patrick Pintaske, Lucy Pittard, Richard Pledge, Alice Pocock, Fiona Pollard, Claire Pompili, Lucy Ponting, Lara Prentice, Natasha Prynne, Faye Pulleyn, Anna Radecka, Syd Rae, Samantha Ranaweera, Kernisha Ransome, Nadia Rasheed, Harriet Reed, Megan Reidy, Natasha Ridley, Barbora Rimkova, Reenell Roach-Williams, Mark Roberts, Pamela Roberts, Elizabeth Roberts, Emma Robinson, Katherine Rogers, Madeleine Ross-Masson, Calista Ross-Peterson, Sophie Rowatt, Megan Rowlands, Sunita Sagoo, Nassima Saidani, Rachel Salenius, Clara Samuel, Kaylee Sanford, Billie Sanger, Marcio Santarosa, Pranav Sarin, Gerda Satunaite, Anna Saunders, Kate Seckington, Wamika Sehgal, Mai Seida, Rabeeah Shah, Melissa Sharpe, Sobia Shatti, Mengqin Shen, Deric Shen, Emma Sheppard, Poonam Shukla, Monika Sievers, Yana Simakova, Rachael Simpson, Gurfateh James Singh, Charlotte Slade, Mark Smith, Charlotte Smith, Lucia Smith, Olivia Broadbent Smith, Rosanna Smith, Chris Smith, Emme Sparre-Slater, Angela Spink, Lorna Stimson, Camelia Sule, Kemi Sulola, Tamanna Sultana, Emma Sutcliffe, Philippa Sutcliffe, Hannah Sutherland, Sarah Sweet, Kazusa Takamura, Angel Tam, Nicola Tattersfield, Poppy Taylor, Matthew Taylor, Molly Taylor, Nicola Teale, Helena Tegeder, Marina Tegeder, Helen Thomas, PK Thummukgool, Kathryn Tickle, Mai Tieu, Beth Tilly, Charlie Todman, Bryony Tofton, Isabelle Tollitt, Billie Towers, Katherine Towerton, Julia Townend, Sekou Traore, Cecile Tremolieres, Louisa Trickett, Gina Trinchese, Anastasia Tsangarides, Melanie Tse, Alice Tucker, Beca Tuffnell, Jonathan Turner, Lisa Valde, Wendy Castano Vega, Sophie Venes, Ruby Vestey, Paul Vincent, Daniel Vincenze, Kalpani Vitharana, Tom Voller, Jana Vrabelova, Angela Wade, Angela Wade, Caroline Walotka, Xiaoyun Wang, Victoria Watson, Jordan Watson, Elizabeth Webb, Jamey-Leigh Weber, Lianna Weidle, Jess Wheelband, Leanne White, Gianne Williams, Naomi Williams, Anna Witcombe, Finola Woolgar, Stephanie Woolven, Ying Wu, Lixiaoxue Xia, Jing Yang, Lanxiubo Yang, Yang Yang, Farhana Yeasmien, Amanda Yuan, Jovana Zarubica, Mona Zaw, Ruth Zewge, Xinyu Zhang, Yiyi Zhao, Min Zhou **Technical Team** Tracy Abercombie, David Adkin, James Adkins, Mauricio Affonso, Ash Ahn, Christopher Amaning, Keren Amroussi, Eleanor Andrews, Nick Ashby, Theo Athanasopoulos, Miles Baldwin, Charlotte Banner, Jonathan Barlow, Andrea Bennett, Paul Bond, Nikki Boone, Bekki Boot, Alastair Borland, Matt Boswood, Rachel Bottomley, Charlotte Boulton, Heather Bourne, Alex Braithwaite, Alex Bratza, Natalie Braune, Chris Brown, Claudia Bryan-Joyce, Jess Buckley, Jarrett Bulat, Mike Burke, Rowan Burton, Elliot Carmichael, Becky Carolan, Kriss Carr, Laura Carus, Pamela Casasa, Danielle Casey, Claire Charlesworth, Tania Clarke, Peter Clerkin, Matthew Compton, Matt Compton, Itziar Coteron, Megan Courage, Lesley Covington, Roz Creusson, Reece Crisp , Moira Cross, Holly Curtis, Anna Czerniawska , Adam Dallman, Merlin Dass, Lee Davies, Christian Davies, Tom Davis, Amanda Derrick, Hannah Dimelow, Stuart Dingley, Ian Dixon-Wilkinson, Ben Donoghue, Grace Douetil, Myfanwy Dowding, Katie Ducarreaux, Alex Durrell, Sasja Ekenberg, Sandra Elsom, Susan Entwistle, Ilse Euser, Gabriella Fewster, Holly Fitch, Nathalie Fitzgerald, Luke Flint, Hazel Frame, Gemma French, Juno Frewing, Laizan Fung, Sean Gallacher, Jimmy Garner-Currie, Jayne Gibson, Sam Gilham, Abi Gill, Lesley Gill, Caroline Gladwin, Phil Gomme, Linda Gray, Adam Gray, Erin Green, Simeon Green, Jamie Grossman, Charlie Hain, Laura Hammond, Kate Harries, Rachel Harris, Iain Harvey, Iyo Hasegawa, Joyce Hastings, Ceri Hazelden, Anthony Holme, Abby Holmes, Chris Howard, Emily Howie, Emma Hughes, Rebecca Humphreys, Hilary Hunt, Amy Insole, Sarah Jackson, Rory Jakeman, Piran Jeffcock, Charlie Johnson, Lisa Juergensen, Maria Kalamara, Helena Kanoute, Jessica Kelley, Francesca Kelly, Marie Kristine Kenmochi, Reese Kirsh, Olivia Alice Knight, Eleftherios Kotsis, Katie Kozlowska, Kemey Lafond, Jennie Leach, Nigel Letheren, Charlotte Levy, Qiming Liu, Tink Lloyd, Chris Lloyd, Edward Locke, Daisy Long, Sam Mannis, Theodora Marlas, Elisabetta Massimi, Hannah McArdle, Jo McDonald, Danielle McNiven, Marta Micallef, Hannah Moore, Josh Moore, Joe Morgan, Rikhil Morjaria, Luke Morton, Luisa Mota, Valerie Munday, Sophie Naisbitt, William Newman, Anna Newton , Anh Hoang Nguyen, James Nicholson , Katy Nixon, Sam Ohlsson, Connaire Packeer, Christina Palaiologou, Amelia Palmer-Johnston, Hannah Pardon, Joe Park, Heather Passmore, Ryan Penny, Alex Peters, Philip Peters, Theresa Pine, Patrick Pintaske, Ellie Pitt, Gareth Prentice, Beth Price Williams, Alison Prior, Will Purton, David Putman, Alex Randall, Joe Ratcliffe, Sonia Razi, Caroline Rechter, Greg Reekie, Yuan Ren , Daisy Rigley, Daniel Roach- Williams, Jonathan Roberts, Thomas Robinson, Tom Robson, Seth Rook Williams, Jack Ryan, Alison Rycroft, Alison Rycroft, Venetia Samuel, Priti Shah, Caroline Sheard, Kathryn Shooter, Jeremy Silverstone, Elliot Sinclair, Sophie Skelton, George Smith, Ollie Smith, Damien Stanton, Hannah Stewart, Sharna Stockdale, Sam Stuart, David Tague, Sabina Tajbhai, Karl Taylor, Ann Taylor, Richard Thurlow, Charlie Todman, George Townsend, Dave Train, Michael Trasmundi, Lucy Vann, James Wakerell, Luke Wallace, Paul Walmsley, Caroline Walotka, Becca Walters, George Walters, Louisa Ward, Shirley Ann Waterhouse, Gina Watson, Amy Watts, Ben Watts , Jenny Webster, Tara Wells, Laura Whitley, Amy Whittle, Paul Williams, Anthony Willis-Osborne, Liz Wimms, Jon Wing, Jonathan Wright, Ben Yager, Noemi Zajzon **Operations Team** Temitope Adetunji, Tryvell Allen-Charles, Nabeel Arshad, Becki Austin, Dandan Bai, Loudmar Bento Portilho, Chris Blackledge, Cormac Bonar, Reece Bourne, Mary Boyes, Jenna Brailey, Doyin Brown, Delphie Callender-Foster, Laura Cantegreil, Jody Chappell, Meng Chen, Tianran Chen, Cheng Cheng, Amy Christie, Lea Clark, Sue Clarke, Christal Clashing O'Reilly, Alexandra Clipa, Nicholas Columbo, Joshua Connolly, Scott Crowhurst, Andrew Davidson, Gemma Davis, Li Ding, Andrea Donigan, Efi Doron, Farid Dudha, Laurene Duret, Katy Earth, Rowanne Eeles, Toby Erskine Crum, Rhea Foy, Mary Furlong, Vanda Galazka, Rosie Gamble, Gus Garcia Lopez, Charmaine Nicole Griffith-McCann, Emma Gyasi, Julie Haggar, Hannah Hand, Emma Hannibal, Coretta Hart, Suchita Hathiramani, Philomena Hayward, Jay Heard, Sophie Heath, Sze Lok Ho, Barbara Hochrath, Danielle Holland, Shan Howes, Minghan Hu, Chen Huang, Jessica Ibeh, Susan Johansson, Akshata Kamath, Tijana Kasic, Ambrosia KejingZhu, Michelle Lacey, Holly Laws, Martina Lee, William Leung, Yee Row Liew, Mei Chern Lim, Henry Lin, Sasha-Louise Lopez, Richard Lorde, Mark Luggar, Laura Macrae, Rob Madeley, Tanisha Malkki, Peter Marley, Shayesteh Mazloumian, Rachel McDermott, Sharon McElhinney, Ambre McGee, Peter McGuinness, Alexander McKinven, Danni Mehta, King Mensah, Saira Mirza, Bryony Mitchison, Kirsty Moss, Hollie Munford, Carol Nascimento, Laura Nastase, Selena Ng, Sian Nicholas, Laura Oakley, Sarah-Jane O'Brien, Dawn O'Brien, Sevda Onder, Hilary Osei-Asibey, Julia Ouzia, Jonny Paim, Viktorija Panfilova, Wai Yee Pang, Louise A Panteli, Franklin Pate, Vaneshaben Patel, Kathy Peacock , Amanda Peck, Zoe Pickburn, Olivia Pole-Evans, Elizabeth Redpath, Alexandra Redpath, Tammy Rennie, Tim Reynolds, Olivia Roach, Niel Robbins, Joanna Rockliff, Sue Rowland, Jack Rule, Lena Ruprai, Nathan Ryan, Kimberley Sayers, Shreeya Shah, Mark Shannon, Bing Sheahan, Matilde Silva, Bhupinder Jit Singh, Aga Spiewak, James Stock, Yuka Tanaka, Kath Tatlock, Jack Tattersall, Alex Taylor, Carol-Ann Tennant, Ruth Tesfai, Emma Thompstone, Vuong Tong, Jeff Tong, Kate Tucker, Edson Sydney Tucker, Andrew van Blommestein, Nancy Vigrass , Benjamin Walker, Gavin Walsh, Charlie Welch, Toni Wong, Jing Zhao, Ji Zhu **Thank you to the following groups who appeared in the Ceremony.** Blackheath Morris, English National Ballet, Hackney Colliery Band, Liverpool Philharmonic Youth Choir, The Liverpool Signing Choir, London Welsh Male Voice Choir, The London Welsh Rugby Club Choir, Rag Morris, The Reading Scottish Pipe Band, The Royal Ballet School, Spelbound, Urban Voices, VP Bhangra **Thank you to the east London Host Borough schools whose pupils appeared in the Ceremony.** Barking Abbey College, Dagenham Park Church of England School, George Greens School, Jo Richardson Community School, Leytonstone School, Little Ilford School, Roding Primary School, Stoke Newington School, Thomas Tallis School, William Ford Church of England Junior School **Thank you to all the Games-time role volunteers who contributed to the delivery of the Ceremony. And thank you to all the drama, dance, music and sports groups, societies, centres, organisations and clubs throughout the UK for all their help and support and for publicising our call for volunteers. We couldn't have done it without you.**

Delivering a memorable Olympic Games to inspire a generation with the support of our Partners

Worldwide Olympic Partners

London 2012 Olympic Partners

London 2012 Olympic Supporters

London 2012 Olympic Suppliers and Providers

Aggreko, Airwave, Atkins, The Boston Consulting Group, CBS Outdoor, Crystal CG, Eurostar, Freshfields Bruckhaus Deringer LLP, G4S, GlaxoSmithKline, Gymnova, Heathrow Airport, Heineken UK, Holiday Inn, John Lewis, McCann Worldgroup, Mondo, NATURE VALLEY, Next, Nielsen, Populous, Rapiscan Systems, Rio Tinto, Technogym, Thames Water, Ticketmaster, Trebor, Westfield.